From Islam to Secular Humanism

*For Zahid
an enlightened
man,
Sohail
June 2006*

From Islam to Secular Humanism

A Philosophical Journey

Dr. K. Sohail

Abbeyfield Publishers
Toronto, Canada

Copyright © 2001 by K. Sohail

All rights reserved. No part of this publication may reproduced or transmitted in any form or by any means, electronic or mechanical, including photocopying, recording, or any information storage and retrieval system, without permission in writing from the author.

Published in 2001 by Abbeyfield Publishers,
a division of The Abbeyfield Companies Ltd.
33 Springbank Avenue, Toronto, Ontario Canada M1N 1G2

Ordering information
Distributed in Canada by Hushion House Distributors Ltd.
36 Northline Road, Toronto, Ontario, Canada M4B 3E2
Phone (416) 285-6100, Fax (416) 285-1777

Cataloguing in Publication Data
Sohail, K. (Khalid), 1952–
 From Islam to secular humanism : a philosophical journey

ISBN 1-894584-07-4

1. Sohail, K. (Khalid), 1952– —Religion. 2. Humanists–Canada–Biography.
3. Muslims—Biography. 4. Spiritual biography. I. Title

BP80.S63 A3 2001   211'.6'092   C2001-930629-6

Cover and textual design: Karen Petherick, Markham, Ontario
Editing: Bill Belfontaine
Book Management: Abbeyfield Consultants, Toronto, Ontario
Printed and bound in Canada by TTP Tradeworx Ltd.

Affectionately dedicated to

my nephew Zeeshan

and

all those who are trying to leave

the highways of tradition

and discover

the trails of their hearts.

acknowledgements

The generosity of spirit shown by my many friends has had a great deal to do with the continuation of my creative, professional and philosophical journey. I will always feel grateful to my uncle, Arif Abdul Mateen, who was a fountain of knowledge and wisdom and a source of inspiration for me all my life.

How writers get along without a dear friend and colleague like Anne Aguirre who made my words and ideas more clear on her computer, is a mystery to me.

I also applaud the creative genius of book designer, Karen Petherick of Intuitive Design International Inc., who has caught the essence of my work so spiritually on a truly inspiring cover and developed the typography and layout on the inner pages and made them so readable.

To Bill Belfontaine of Abbeyfield Publishers, who managed the project and kept an experienced eye upon details, I extend my profound thanks.

milestones

Foreword	xiii
Introduction	1
From the Womb of Islam	5
Religion and Science ~ Part One	15
Religion and Politics	29
Religion and Science ~ Part Two	41
Religion and Mysticism	55
Siddhartha ~ A Symbol of Spiritual Journey	83
Krishnamurti ~ A Symbol of Freedom	95
Insanity and Spirituality	113
Mystic Poetry	125
Secular Humanism	139
Dreamers	159

foreword

Dear Sohail,

How wonderfully you have shared your spiritual journey with youthful readers and particularly with your nephew Zeeshan—and hopefully with many older readers. You shared the importance of "the trail of the heart" and the family tradition of choosing "the non-traditional path." This has personal meaning to me, for in my life I have also made the searching my primary aim.

When I was a youth in China, about age 16, the famous British Sinologist Joseph Needham was invited to speak at the university in Chengdu on the 400th anniversary of the birth of Copernicus. It's interesting as I look back, to realize how deeply I was influenced by his words. He started off similarly to your journey, although in his case his orientation was High Anglicanism. As he delved into science and particularly the physics of matter and energy, his belief in God dissolved, and became quite meaningless and irrelevant. But within the formation and structure of matter he began to perceive a continuous pattern or process, which saw parts forming ever more complex structures. I cannot convey the details but he traced the formation of matter from the big bang through all the stages up to molecules, living cells, more and more complex life forms, right up to the 70 to 100 trillion celled human being. Detecting something enormously fascinating about this creative tendency in matter, Needham rediscovered faith on an entirely new level. If for billions of years more and more complex harmonies of parts were verifiable to the eyes of science, faith for Needham was reborn. At that point Needham coincided almost exactly with your conclusions: "I hope that...we decide to discover new ways of living harmoniously with ourselves, other human beings, and Mother Nature". This had enormous meaning for Needham—he believed that the process of harmonization of parts into larger wholes had proceeded inevitably until humans, with as you term it, the ability "to know that they know" and to make choices, arrived. For the first time the unfolding of creation contained a self-conscious element with choice and Needham at this point regained his faith. He believed that whatever lay behind this unfolding possibility for parts to become subsumed into larger wholes was God and that the process of assisting this process was "the will of God".

I have to share the above, for in my journey I find meaning in assisting this process in whatever way I can. My favourite analogy is with the evolution of an orchestra. The soloist first masters self-expression. Later in the mystery of the orchestra, the soloist asks, "Can I play what I wish, when I wish, the way I wish—the free way I'm used to playing as a soloist?"—and the conductor kindly but firmly says, "No, the rules of playing in an orchestra are that you take your lead from the conductor. In this way you become part of a larger whole. You may continue to be a soloist with total freedom of self-expression and at the same time experience what it is to be part of a larger whole, a whole larger than the sum of all the parts." This analogy has some bearing for us in a world crammed with soloists. And in the nineteenth century, before an international agreement made A 440 the universally accepted tuning standard for all pianos and musical instruments, orchestras from different countries would have been unable to play together without a total distortion of the composer's music. It was this that led me to the Baha'i faith, which is much more like the composition of a human orchestra playing the highest ideals and values of all past religious manifestations. We have no churches, preachers or conscience pressures imposed on us from above.

Sohail, these are personal reflections of my own which in no way detract from your manuscript. I began to read it the night we met and after some delays, which I regret, I finished reading it recently. I started making notes but later read rather avidly, wanting to follow all the many facets of your spiritual journey. You write sincerely, gently and eloquently from the heart and like all pioneers who have extracted truth from experience, your focus is on what unfolds—not on the reactions of those rigidly committed to the "gods" of past human fabrications.

Grateful for your sharing,

Omar Walmsley
Muskoka, Canada

From Islam to Secular Humanism

Introduction

My philosophical, spiritual and ideological journey from Islam to Secular Humanism has been long and convoluted, at times painful, at other times adventurous. I experienced many breakdowns and breakthroughs along the way. When I reminisce about the last three decades of my life, I remember:

... the time when I believed in Islam and considered myself a dedicated Muslim.

... the period when I was full of doubts and conflicts and experienced an intellectual nightmare.

... the phase when I was disillusioned with the institution of organized religion

and

... a stage when I found myself in a spiritual no-man's land.

In the last decade of my life I feel:

... my travels in North America, Europe, the Middle East, South Africa and South America.

... my studies in Mystic and Wisdom Literature and translating World Literature into Urdu.

... my interviews with Asian writers living in the East and the West

and

... my journey of self-discovery and soul-searching has helped me grow to the next stage of my life where I firmly believe in Secular Humanism.

Articulating one's life philosophy is not an easy task especially for me, knowing very well that I am still changing and growing. (I hope I keep on until the day I die.)

Being a writer, I am well aware of the limitation of words. I feel they do not do justice to our ideas and experiences. But in these essays I will share with you some of the highlights of my ideological growth and milestones of my philosophical journey. They will communicate the essence of the metamorphosis I went through in my adult life. My words are affectionate extensions of my SELF, hoping to touch and embrace those I may never meet in person because of our geographical and temporal distances and ideological differences. I believe in a genuine dialogue as it reflects a democratic spirit and a genuine desire to learn and grow. This book is not written to offend or hurt anyone. I hope my readers receive these essays with the same affection and regard as they are offered. Human minds are like parachutes; they work only when they are open.

K. Sohail

*From the Womb
of Islam*

When I reminisce about my childhood, I remember growing up in a traditional, conservative and religious family, surrounded by a traditional Islamic culture. My parents and their families emigrated from Amritsar to Lahore, from India to Pakistan in 1947. They were proud that they became citizens of the biggest Muslim state in the world, the only country on the map that was born from the womb of Islam. They were thrilled that they would get an opportunity to live in a Muslim culture far away from the Hindus, Sikhs and Parsis of India.

In my biofictional story, *Mother Earth Is Sad*, I have narrated the story of their emigration in the voice of my grandmother:

> "My sister and brother left for Lahore and wanted me and the children to join them but I stayed behind and waited for your grandfather.
> Every day that passed
> seemed like a decade
> every night like a century.
> Finally
> when your grandfather arrived,

we decided to leave.
With empty hands
we moved on.
We left behind
our property,
the business
and a furnished home.

Your grandfather had a good friend who used to look after us when he was away. He loved us and we trusted him. The day we decided to move, your grandfather's friend went to get us a taxi so that we could go to the railway station; he never came back.

We waited impatiently for him for an hour, and then another, until finally three hours or more had passed. When he did not return we realized he had been killed by a sword, a kirpan or a gun.

So your grandfather went out himself to get a taxi. It was a risky affair. Halfway he met a Sardarji, his childhood buddy.

'Khawaja Sahib! Where are you going?' he asked.

'To get a taxi for the children.'

'Don't go any further. If you approach the four corners you will be killed. Go back. I will try my best to get a taxi.'

After a few minutes he came with a taxi, hid us in it and took us to the railway station.

When we arrived at the station we found that the train had been waiting for the past forty-eight hours. The driver was afraid to leave the station as he did not want the train ambushed and the passengers killed. People were clinging to the train like bees to the honeycomb. They were jammed into the seats, huddled on the floor, clutching onto the footsteps and hanging precariously from the windows. We asked the children to wait, perhaps for a miracle, for surely a miracle was needed to transport us from the dangers of Amritsar to the safety of Lahore.

After twenty-four agonizing hours of waiting, we heard the train whistle blow, announcing the departure. Your grandfather had a dangerous but novel idea. "Why don't we travel on the roof," he asked and we all clambered on top of the shoulders of other cursing passengers, up to the roof of the train, risking our lives in doing so.

The train left the station and started to crawl cautiously, as if afraid. It was terrifying as we slowly moved toward the border. We covered a two-hour journey in twelve hours. When we arrived at the Lahore station everybody was relieved to have escaped what seemed like a death sentence. Your grandfather and I had tears in our eyes. Mine were tears of joy, happy that my children had been saved, his were tears of sadness, as he had lost his friend. That loss wounded your grandfather's heart. It was a wound that never healed. That immigration was painful and heartbreaking. It was like crossing a river;

    a river of blood,

    a river of fire,

    a river of divided loyalties

    broken faiths

    and shattered dreams.

Some stayed behind,

From Islam to Secular Humanism

some drowned halfway

and some arrived at the other shore.

We would never know for sure what we had lost and what we had gained on that journey."

My parents had an arranged marriage in 1950 and I was born into a happy household two years later. In 1954, when my dad passed his Masters Examination in Mathematics, he was offered a job at Government College in Kohat, Pakistan. At the age of two I moved with my parents from Lahore to Kohat, not only to a different city but also a different province and culture. People all around us spoke Pushto while my parents did not understand a word of it. I can imagine the difficulties they must have had to adjust to a traditional tribal culture, especially when my mother rarely, if ever, left our home.

The difficulties, struggles and challenges became so stressful that my father had a nervous breakdown when I was about ten years old.

I remember the day when, after frantically pacing back and forth in his room throughout the night, he finally lost control and started shouting out meaningless torrents of words. My mother called one of his friends who took him to the hospital. He was so out of control that he required restraint. His hands and feet were tied to the bed. While the doctors and the nurses were trying to control him, I remember sitting on a windowsill in the next room praying to God for help and strength. After a few days, his struggles lessened to the point that he was sent to Lahore to be with my mother's family who looked after him day and night for months. They had planned the nursing care in four-hour shifts so as not to leave him alone, because he surely would have done himself serious injury or fled, never to be found. The unfortunate thing was that the family would not let me see him, as they were apprehensive what he might do to me. Yet, my love for my father was more powerful than their wish to keep me away. I crept quietly into his room. He hugged and kissed me and talked to me so very affectionately with tears in his eyes. How could I know fear from this kind man?

I remember one evening though, when he was climbing up the stairs to the roof and I was following, he stopped on the last step and started talking to the stars. That day I came to realize that there was something wrong with him but still that did not make me nervous.

When he finally recovered a few months later, he was a changed man. He had gone through a mysterious and mystical transformation. Everybody thought he had had a total nervous breakdown which left him seriously handicapped because he was so unlike the husband and father he was before, but he believed he had achieved a most wonderful breakthrough. He became quite a religious person. Although my mother was pleased that he had recovered, she was disappointed to find out that he no longer wanted to teach at the college. That was quite stressful for her and it became her turn to be physically and mentally sick. He accepted a job teaching in a high school and family moved back to Peshawar, in the Pukhtoon culture.

From Islam to Secular Humanism

In Peshawar, I remember both my parents
... reciting Quran daily
... praying regularly
... observing fasts every year
... paying zakaat (charity)

and praying to go to Mecca, the holiest of holy places, one day to perform Haj, the pilgrimage. Both my parents tried their best to provide a religious atmosphere for my upbringing. My mother started teaching me Quran when I was only four and encouraged me to fast and pray when I reached the age of seven. By the time I was eleven, I had finished all thirty chapters of Quran in Arabic. They succeeded in making me a dedicated and devoted Muslim like themselves. My dad felt so exuberant with the spirit of Islam that he added the name Mohammad to my legal name, Khalid Sohail, when I was twelve, without discussing it with me.

In 1965 Pakistan had a war with India that lasted for seventeen days. Blackouts became a regular feature every night. I saw bombs dropped that murdered and mutilated innocent people in villages. People became very religious and fanatic and developed a burning hatred for Hindus that has not abated even today. I was so affected by the war at the age of thirteen that I used to fantasize about joining the army and becoming part of the Islamic Armed Forces. I was taught that Hindus were our enemies and it was sacred to kill them as we were fighting a Jihad, a holy war. We were also told by religious leaders that anyone who is killed in the holy war is a *shaheed* and goes directly to heaven.

During my adolescence, I became very perturbed by the social circumstances I was living in. Whenever I observed my neighbors and friends, I felt distressed at seeing so many suffering and leading miserable lives. I was continually upset to see:

... many children who had no food, clothes or shelter.

... many teenagers who had no money to attend school.

... many wives who were beaten by their husbands on a regular basis.

... many elderly who had no money to see a doctor *and*

... many mentally ill people of all ages who were homeless and walking the streets naked, followed by stray dogs.

When I asked my elders why there was so much suffering everywhere, they told me, "We are not good enough Muslims, we do not follow the teachings of our religion."

There was a time in my life when I believed in a Personal God and respected the teachings of the Prophets and Scriptures like other Muslims and never questioned Miracles and Angels. I was sure that I would be blessed and go to Heaven when I died. I felt sorry for all those who had never heard of Islam or accepted its teachings. For a while I even joined a religious group that traveled from door to door preaching the teachings of Islam and inviting people to mosque for prayers and religious sermons. I felt despair and sorrow for all those Muslims who were so intoxicated with the materialistic world that they paid little or no attention to their religious duties. Many times I arose at three a.m. in the darkness of early morning to offer special prayers of Tahajjad to purify my soul and to pray to God to convert the entire world to Islam.

K. Sohail

Religion and Science

PART ONE

Being brought up in a very traditional and religious family and a conservative culture, I found myself at a crossroads when I started to study Science. My inner conflict reached its climax when I entered medical school and started studying anatomy, physiology, biochemistry and embryology. It did not take me long to realize that Science was more than facts and figures and statistics, it was also a unique attitude, and a special way of seeing, analyzing and understanding life. It was a philosophy; but that scientific philosophy was not only different, it was contradictory to the religious philosophy I had been imbued with from an early age. The scientific knowledge was a continual challenge and a threat to the belief system that I had inherited from my ancestors.

Being a traditional Muslim, I believed in a personal God, in miracles, in prayers, in life after death and in the teachings of prophets and scriptures. But the Science I was studying was encouraging me to follow rational thought rather than blind faith. Science was focusing on the observations made by the microscope and the telescope, rather than on the divine revelations of the scriptures. Those two philosophies, the scientific and the religious, were creating havoc not only in my inquiring mind, but in my heart and soul that believed so strongly in the virtues of Islam. That continuing conflict led to sleepless nights and I went through a turbulent phase in my adolescence that I identified as an "extended intellectual nightmare."

One of the tragedies was that my teachers of science and medicine in the university had little interest or in-depth knowledge of religion and scriptures; and the religious leaders I knew had no sound knowledge or understanding of the fundamentals of Science. Science and Religion were two banks of the river in the cultural flow I grew up in, existing opposite each other but never coming together. Trying to find a bridge between the two banks, one of Science and the other of Religion (which for me was Islam), I consulted libraries and immersed myself in books of great variety. The first group of religious writers, intellectuals and scholars I explored, were Abul Aala Maududi, Ghulam Ahmed Pervaiz, Mohammad Iqbal and Abul Kalaam Aazaad. These authors had written about those issues seriously and had expressed their views very clearly. Their writings opened new doors and took me into rooms of awareness and I realized how unfortunate it was for me to be a Muslim and not even know the basics of Arabic. As I could not read Quran and Hadees, the sayings of Mohammed directly, I had to rely on translations and interpretations.

For me the biggest conflict was the role of an omnipotent and omnipresent, all powerful God in our day-to-day lives. I was a believer in miracles and prayers. I had observed Muslims gathering in Eid Gah Mosque to offer Salaat-e-Hajat (special prayers) to make rain. Yet here was Science inviting me to explore the relationship between cause and effect, teaching me that everything that happens all around us has a reason, and that the role of Science is to explore those reasons so that it brings us to realize that there is a rational understanding of life.

According to the teachings of Islam, angels were appointed by God to perform different duties:

an angel for revelation...Gibraeel.

an angel for winds and rain...Michaeel.

an angel for death...Izraeel.

an angel to announce "Qiamat",

the Day of Judgement... Israfeel.

The role of those angels was a mystery for me as a student of Science. Science was teaching me that all events in our lives, whether sunrise, eclipse, starlight, childbirth, illness or death, could be understood by scientific laws. I remember feeling relieved when I read that Ghulam Ahmed Pervaiz had translated the Quranic expression *malaika* as "laws of nature" (qawaneen-e-fitrat), in his book M*af hum-ul-Quran*, rather than "angels" (farishtay) as many other scholars had translated over the centuries. Pervaiz was attempting in his writings to encourage a rational attitude towards Quran and Islam. He believed that all encounters with life could be divided into three parts:

From Islam to Secular Humanism

Rational part: those encounters that can be understood through logical and analytical thinking. They belong to the scientific world.

Irrational part: those encounters that are illogical and cannot be understood according to scientific laws.

Ultra-rational part: those encounters that can neither be proved or disproved by logical thinking. Like the ultra-violet rays of the sun, they are beyond the range of rationality. Pervaiz believed that concepts of God and life after death could be included in the Ultra-rational part and that they belonged to the religious world, while miracles like conception without a sperm and an ovum belonged to the Irrational world. He did not believe in such miracles.

The second discovery for me was when I read Iqbal's lectures entitled, *Reconstruction of Religious Thought in Islam*. In those lectures Iqbal suggested that we read Quranic expressions as symbolic and metaphorical rather than making literal interpretations. He believed that "heaven" and "hell" were "states" not "places", and the Quranic and Biblical story of Adam and Eve was a story representing Man and Woman, rather than individuals. Reading scriptures and interpreting them in a metaphorical way was a giant step in my intellectual and philosophical evolution. After that, I could read scriptures as a part of literature, folklore and mythology. It was a major breakthrough in my philosophical struggles. It helped me understand that many conflicts between Religion and Science were the result of literal interpretations of the scriptures.

During my studies of medicine and embryology I was

also fascinated with Darwin's theory of evolution. I was quite puzzled that most Muslim scholars, even Abul Aala Maududi, rejected the theory of evolution and believed it contradicted the Quranic theory of Creation. The only Muslim scholar that I found who accepted Darwin's theory and did not see it in conflict with Quran was Abul Kalaam Aazaad. In his interpretation of Quranic verses in his book *Tarjaman-ul-Quran*, he translated the Quranic expression "nafs-un-wahida" as unicellular organism rather than a human Adam like most other scholars. He also developed from different Quranic verses how life on earth started in the oceans and then went through different stages of evolution. It was impressive for me as a student of embryology to read how he highlighted that a human zygote passes through all stages of evolution during nine months of development in the mother's womb.

Those studies and interpretations of Quran were a mixed blessing for me. On one hand they showed me that Quran could be read in a way that it did not conflict with modern scientific discoveries, but it also showed me how subjective those interpretations could be. Different scholars, depending on their philosophies and biases, could arrive at different interpretations and understandings of the same verses. After that study, the Holy Books seemed more literary pieces of human history reflecting the cultural psyche of the communities that gave birth to those scriptures, than "cook-book recipes" for day to day living or books of law to make constitutions or penal codes for religious nations.

After reading the works of Muslim scholars, I tried to study other world religions and read books written by Western scholars to become acquainted with their views.

Of all those scholars whose works I read, I would like to discuss two.

The first is Bertrand Russell. When I read his book, *Why I am Not A Christian*, it was really an eye-opener for me. I had never read any other intellectual who was as open, honest and straightforward as Russell. He was an atheist and was of the opinion that all religions were dangerous for human civilization. He did not mince words.

> "*I think all the great religions of the world—Buddhism, Hinduism, Christianity, Islam and Communism—are both untrue and harmful. It is evident as a matter of logic that, since they disagree, not more than one of them can be true.*" (Ref. 1, p. V)

Russell's thoughts were a shock to my system. When I tried to understand his criticisms and objections to the world religions, especially Christianity, my mind was filled to overflowing with provocative ideas. I would like to share a few of them.

Being an atheist, Russell did not believe in God, in an omnipotent, omnipresent Creator of the universe. He was quite sarcastic in expressing his point of view.

> "*Do you think that, if you were granted omnipotence and omniscience and millions of years in which to perfect your*

world, you could produce nothing better than the Ku Klux Klan or the Fascists?" (Ref. 1, p. 10)

Russell also believed that not only has Religion retarded human progress, growth and evolution, it has also been a cause of many holy wars and acts of cruelty.

"In the so-called ages of faith, when men really did believe the Christian religion in all its completeness, there was the Inquisition, with the tortures, there were millions of unfortunate women burned as witches, and there was every kind of cruelty practised upon all sorts of people in the name of religion...I say quite deliberately that the Christian religion, as organized in its churches, has been and still is the principal enemy of moral progress in the world." (Ref. 1, p. 21).

Russell was critical not only of the concept of God and institutionalized religion, he was also critical of Christ because Christ believed in Hell and eternal damnation for those who did not accept his message. Russell had more regard for Socrates and Buddha than Christ, as they did not believe in Hell.

"There is one very serious defect to my mind in Christ's moral character, and that is that He believed in hell. I do not myself feel that any person who is really profoundly humane can believe in everlasting punishment."..."You will find that in the Gospels Christ said, 'Ye serpents, Ye

From Islam to Secular Humanism

generation of vipers, how can Ye escape the damnation of hell'. That was said to people who did not like His preaching." (Ref. 1, p. 17)

"I really do not think that a person with a proper degree of kindliness in his nature would have put fears and terrors of that sort into the world." (Ref. 1, p. 18)

One of the major objections Russell had about all religions and religious institutions and governments was that they controlled children's minds through religious education. Those religious institutions were a hindrance to natural and free development of people's minds because they encouraged blind faith rather than critical and logical thinking.

"The conviction that it is important to believe this or that, even if a free inquiry would not support the belief, is one which is common to almost all religions and which inspires all systems of state education. The consequence is that the minds of the young are stunted and are filled with fanatical hostility both to those who have other fanaticisms and, even more virulently, to those who object to all fanaticisms." (Ref. 1, p. vi)

It was ironic that Russell, who always supported free education, became victim of religious hostility and prejudice when he was offered a position as Professor of Philosophy in the State of New York.

K. Sohail

When Russell's appointment became public, Bishop Manning of the Protestant Episcopal Church wrote a letter to all New York newspapers in which he denounced the board's action.

> *"What is to be said of colleges and universities which hold up before our youth as a responsible teacher of philosophy...a man who is a recognized propagandist against both religion and morality...and who specifically defends adultery..."* (Ref. 1, p. 209).

The Bishop's letter created such a negative public opinion that Russell's offer was withdrawn and he was persecuted and penalized for his personal beliefs which had nothing to do with his competence to be a professor of philosophy. It was interesting for me to read that Russell, in spite of his respect and fame as a scientist and mathematician, was not allowed to teach "in the land of the free" because of his personal morals and views.

The second Western scholar that I found quite intellectually stimulating was Sigmund Freud. Freud, from a Jewish background, was also critical of Religion and considered it an illusion, but he was not as aggressive in his approach as Russell. Freud considered religious beliefs as illusions because "Religious ideas are teachings and assertions about facts and conditions of external (or internal) reality which tell one something one has not discovered for oneself and which lay claim to one's belief." (Ref. 2, p. 25)

From Islam to Secular Humanism

Freud even went a step further than illusion and wrote, "Religion would thus be the universal obsessional neurosis of humanity..." (Ref. 2, p. 43)

Like Russell, Freud was aware that religious beliefs had such a hold in people's cultural psyche that if people criticized or challenged those beliefs with Science and logical thinking they would be punished, penalized and persecuted. He wrote thus about the teachings of Religion,

> *"When we ask on what their claim to be believed is founded, we are met with three answers, which harmonize remarkably badly with one another. Firstly, these teachings deserve to be believed because they were already believed by our primal ancestors, secondly, we possess proofs which have been handed down to us from those primeval times, and thirdly, it is forbidden to raise the question of their authentication at all. In former days anything so presumptuous was visited with the severest penalties, and even today society looks askance at any attempt to raise the question again."* (Ref. 2, p. 26)

Freud was optimistic that as Science enlarged its territories, Religion would have no choice but to withdraw. He was hopeful that in the long run logical thought would triumph over blind faith. He believed Religion was a phenomenon of the past while the future belonged to Science.

K. Sohail

"The scientific spirit brings about a particular attitude towards worldly matters; before religious matters it pauses for a little, hesitates, and finally there too crosses the threshold. In this process there is no stopping; the greater the number of men to whom the treasures of knowledge become accessible, the more widespread is the falling-away from religious belief—at first only from its obsolete and objectionable trappings but later from its fundamental postulates as well." (Ref. 2, p. 38)

As I studied different scientists I became aware of the significance of the scientific attitude towards life. I realized that in a culture where people are superstitious and are always waiting for divine intervention to solve their personal, social and political problems, it is important to encourage people to develop an analytical attitude. Such an attitude helps people to view their life events critically, take responsibility for their actions and find ways to solve their own problems.

I feel that for communities and nations to be proud of their scientific discoveries in biological, psychological and anthropological disciplines, schools, colleges, universities and other social institutions have to develop an atmosphere where logical, rational and analytical thinking is respected and promoted. Without such an environment it is not realistic to expect scientific breakthroughs in any aspect of life. (See References on Page 54)

From Islam to Secular Humanism

Religion and Politics

The war with India in 1965 affected me so deeply that I gradually began taking an interest in the relationship between Religion and Politics. Although I was never a member of any political party, yet living in a politically unstable and religiously fanatic part of the world, it was almost impossible not to be affected by the political and religious changes in my environment and to develop strong reactions to them.

In October 1968, President Ayub Khan had celebrated ten years of Basic Democratic Rule in Pakistan. He was quite well liked and respected in the first few years of his rule but gradually as he became the administrator of martial law, his policies became more dictatorial and his sons became infamous because of their corruption. Respect for this "saviour" of Pakistan soon deteriorated.

After the war, Zulfiqar Ali Bhutto gradually became so popular that he announced a political party and named it Pakistan People's Party. He became chairman and started making speeches against Ayub Khan's rule. Bhutto talked about the rights of people and establishing democracy in the country. It was ironic that Bhutto had become popular because of Ayub Khan, the same leader he wanted to overthrow. Ayub Khan had appointed him as foreign minister and proudly sent him to the United Nations where he received the world's attention because of his passionate speeches. At twenty-seven he became famous as the world's youngest foreign minister.

Ayub Khan tried to ignore the Pakistan People's Party but Bhutto's firey speeches and charming personality had won people to his cause. I remember listening to his mesmerizing speech for three hours in Shahi Bagh in Peshawar and thoroughly enjoying it, but when I got home and my father asked me what message he had delivered, I was lost for words. That day I realized that although he had talked for hours, he had said nothing significant. People were in love with his charismatic personality. Finally Ayub Khan became so overwhelmed and threatened by Bhutto's popularity that he gave in. The whole country had sunk into a mood of anger and despair. People became so angry with Ayub Khan that when I heard a procession shouting "Ayub Kutta Haiy Haiy" (Shame on Ayub Khan. He is a dog), I felt sorry for him. That day I realized that power was temporary in life. The same man who was respected and adored everywhere a few years earlier was facing public humiliation. Finally Ayub Khan could not survive the pressure of criticism and hate. He stepped down and handed over the government to Field Marshal Yahya Khan who promised to hold free democratic elections in six months.

To the great surprise of many, free elections took place

in December 1970 and for the first time in the history of the country, a political promise was fulfilled. But it turned out to be a mixed blessing. On one hand it gave people hope of living in a democratic society but on the other hand it brought unresolved political and social conflicts to the surface.

When the results of the elections were announced, Bhutto had won the majority vote in West Pakistan while Mujib-ur-Rahman of the Awami League, a great supporter of the Bengali language and culture, had won the majority vote in East Pakistan. Since East Pakistan was the biggest province, constitutionally Majib-ur-Rahman should have been Prime Minister of the whole country, something that Bhutto did not want.

Tensions between East and West Pakistan started to escalate. Finally the army, under the command of General Tikka Khan, was sent to Dacca, the future capital of Bangladesh (East Pakistan). East Pakistan, frustrated and disillusioned with West Pakistan, asked India to help. The crisis took a different turn when on December 17, 1972, the Pakistani army after a long, violent struggle lost the war and a new nation by the name of Bangladesh appeared on the map of the world. The independence of Bangladesh coincided with 90,000 Pakistani soldiers becoming prisoners of war in India, and later on the establishment of Bihari camps in Dacca holding thousands of non-Bengalis who were not in favour of Bangladesh, and who wanted to emigrate to Pakistan. The dream of a united Islamic State finally shattered.

The separation of Bangladesh made it easier for Bhutto to acquire every political power. He subsequently became Prime Minister of Pakistan.

After becoming the head of the state of former West Pakistan, now called Pakistan, it did not take Bhutto long to realize that he was going to face serious political problems in the country because his popularity was mostly in Punjab and Sindh and not in Balochistan and Frontier Province. With the division of a united Pakistan, it was imaginable for other provinces to gain independence too. Tariq Ali had asked a serious question in the form of a book, *Can Pakistan Survive*? People were realizing that Abul Kalaam Aazaad's prediction might come true. He believed that if Muslims and Hindus could not live together in a united India, and if Pakistan was created on the basis of Religion, then after a few decades it might further divide on the basis of language, ethnicity and culture.

The birth of Bangladesh had proven that for different nations to live harmoniously and resolve conflicts, language played a significant role. Mohammad Ali Jinnah's insistence that Bengalis learn Urdu as the national language had backfired. It had created hostility and finally led to having two national languages. Ironically, none of the provinces used Urdu as their native language. They spoke Sindhi, Balochi, Punjabi and Pushto as their mother tongues. People wondered why Pakistan could not include all of them as national languages so that each province could conduct their official business in their mother tongue and children could be taught in their mother tongue in schools. In Pakistan, Urdu had a unique position. It was everybody's language and nobody's language. It was a bridge between four provinces yet none of the provinces owned it. In spite of being a national language, it was not a mother tongue of any of the provinces.

After the independence of Bangladesh, the political tensions and rivalries between the four provinces escalated. Punjab being the biggest province and Punjabi being closest to Urdu, made it possible for Punjab to have more political power than the other provinces. It was not very long before natives of the other provinces started resenting Punjab. They wanted the same rights and privileges as the people of Punjab.

Bhutto had won people's hearts by offering them dreams of Roti-Kapra-Makaan (Food, Clothes, Homes). Using slogans like,

"Islam is our Religion"

"Democracy is our politics"

"Socialism is our economics"

he had tried to bring left wing intellectuals as well as those from the right wing under his flag. Bhutto soon realized that his comrades did not have enough knowledge, wisdom or political insight to help him solve complex socio-political problems that the nation was facing. Bhutto's slogans about Islam, Democracy and Socialism also showed his lack of clarity of thought at a conceptual and philosophical level. They were very confusing for many intellectuals and heavily criticized.

Bhutto's lack of popularity in Balochistan and Frontier

From Islam to Secular Humanism

Province was a major handicap for his party. Being a resident of Frontier Province I was aware of the religious and cultural traditions of Pukhtoons.

In Frontier Province a tug of war existed between competing politicians and political parties:

Qayyum Khan of the Muslim League.

Wali Khan of the National Awami Party.

Mufti Mahmood and Ghulam Ghaus Hazarvi of Jamiat-e-ulama, and Sher Pau of the People's Party.

The popularity of Jamiat-e-ulama, the religious party, can be highlighted by one event. Bhutto who contested elections from five constituencies and won in four leading with thousands of votes, lost in Frontier Province. He was competing against Mufti Mahmood. Mufti Mahmood won ten thousand votes more than Bhutto. People in other provinces were shocked at the results. It was interesting though, how the religious party had won those votes. People from the religious party traveled from door to door with the Quran in their hands, and asked a simple question: "Are you going to vote Quran or Bhutto?"

The simple people did not understand the hidden poison in that simple question. They were gullible and wanted to show their devotion so they voted for Quran which meant Mufti Mahmood. When the votes were counted on election day, Mufti Mahmood won by a significant majority.

Living in Peshawar I also had an opportunity to experience something extraordinary, the speech of Bacha Khan.

Bacha Khan who was Wali Khan's father sat in exile in Afghanistan for more than two decades. He was very critical of Mohammad Ali Jinnah, the founder of Pakistan, and the birth of Pakistan. People called him Gandhi of Sarhad while he called himself Khudai Khitmatgar (A humble servant of the people). I remember the day when the big procession of millions of people and thousands of buses brought Bacha Khan back to his motherland in Pakistan. He made a long and passionate speech in Peshawar. I was amazed that even at the age of ninety he seemed strong and forceful not only in his voice but also in his ideas. He was open and honest in expressing his views and criticisms of Jinnah and the state of Pakistan. Bacha Khan was a great supporter of Pukhtoonistan. He did not understand why the other three provinces had their identities based on their nationalities: Punjab for Punjabis, Sindh for Sindhis, Balochistan for Balochis, but when Pukhtoons wanted to name their province Pukhtoonistan, rather than a sterile name NWFP (North West Frontier Province, a name given by the British) they were called "traitor" by other provinces.

It was also interesting that Bacha Khan, who was considered a traitor by many Pakistanis, was declared a Prisoner of Conscience by Amnesty International.

In spite of the underlying tensions, Bhutto had been successful in bringing a breath of fresh air into the suffocating political climate of Pakistan and had given people the opportunity to dream of a better future. Even the expatriates living in foreign countries had started looking at their homeland with new hopes and some of them seriously considered going back to serve their motherland, the motherland that had treated them as stepchildren for decades.

In my biofictional story *Mother Earth Is Sad* I tried to capture that moment in history.

"It was when all hope seemed lost, that a new chapter started in the history of this land. It was a new beginning and appeared nothing short of a miracle.

It was the movement of the populace.
Masses of people awakened.
The people crowed into the streets.
Lips that had been sealed, opened once more.
Bruised swollen tongues, began to sing.
The poor
    the deprived
        the underprivileged
            the minority groups,
                started to protest.

They began to fight for their rights.

There was an atmosphere of hope, ambition and desire. It was a dream-like state that made us feel like we were floating in the air.

During that time, all the sons and daughters of the motherland who were living in exile and had adopted another country as their motherland, were invited back. They were reassured that their lives and beliefs would be respected. They realized that they were still bound to their mother and motherland with a delicate thread, the remains of their umbilical cord."

But that dream-like state failed to last and the nation awoke to the harsh realities of religious changes implemented by the Bhutto government.

The first step was banning alcohol.

The second was declaring Friday a holiday (holy day) rather than Sunday.

The third and final act was declaring Ahmedis to be non-Muslims. That really broke the hearts of many liberal and left-leaning people and intellectuals who had favoured Bhutto in elections. It was obvious Bhutto had become a puppet in the hands of those who wanted to turn Pakistan into an Islamic State.

That was when I decided to leave Pakistan. For me religion and politics was a dangerous combination. It gave government too much power. Atheists could be declared *murtad* (non-believers) and traitors and killed. I saw so many of my Ahmedi friends who were persecuted and tortured by the right wing religious fanatics. The house of our Ahmedi teachers was burnt by students. I was one of those who protested against religious intolerance. But I was aware that such protests could lead to losing my mind or going to jail. I have shared these views and feelings in detail in my biofictional story A *Stranger in One's Homeland*.

After I left the country, the political situation got worse. Zia-ul-Haq took over, Pakistan became the Islamic Republic of Pakistan and Bhutto was hanged.

From Islam to Secular Humanism

Religion and Science

PART TWO

After reading many Western scholars of Christian and Jewish backgrounds, I tried to expand my philosophical horizons by reading South American and African writers to get their views on Religion and Science. I was quite shocked to read the outrage of African writer Wole Soyinka against Islam and Christianity. He believed that African nations had been colonized by Europe and the Middle East religiously, politically and economically. He thought that getting rid of those foreign influences was crucial for African nations to rediscover their identity and regain their intellectual, artistic and spiritual freedom.

> *"Taken together, therefore, the history of African people provides us with two principal enemies of their authentic traditions and their will to cultural identity. One is European imperialism, the other Arab-Islamic penetration and domination of significant areas of the continent."* (Ref. 3, p. 124)

> *...Freedom remains the antithesis of power, that historically proven corollary of enslavement. Obviously power can*

only be made manifest with the act of enslavement of some other. What then of the Third World, captive and client of the two ideological estates—socialism and capitalism— even as it has been, and still holds itself in thrall to two other alien contending religions, Christianity and Islam? Both these religions in their turn operate globally in mind-boggling, fluctuating alliances with the two main ideological scaffoldings, left and right, yet constantly strike out in their own specific authoritarian-isms, often of the most destructive, anti-humanist nature." (Ref. 3, p. 210)

Wole Soyinka finally asks his people some disturbing questions:

"Are we doomed forever to await the coming-to-terms of these various fountain-heads, with their own contradictions, their own self-deceits, granting them an eternity of aggressive certitudes, conceding the substitution of 'revelationary' for 'scientific' impregnabilities? Are we permanent prisoners of other Berlin Walls that we have actually assisted others in building around ourselves?" (Ref. 3, p. 210)

One of the other writers that attracted my attention was Octavio Paz. Although he was Mexican, he had lived in North America, Europe and India for long periods of time and had tried to incorporate and analyze different cultural and religious traditions in his essays. I was quite intrigued when he compared the battle of Religion and Science in Christian and Muslim worlds. He was of the belief that in the Christian world, Science had won and Christian intellectuals and philosophers, in Nietzche's words had declared "God is Dead"; but on the other hand in the Islamic world, God had won and Science had lost.

> "...Islam has experienced difficulties similar to those Christianity has undergone. Finding it impossible to discover any rational or philosophical ground for belief in a single God, Abu Hamid Ghazali writes his Incoherence of Philosophy; a century later, Averroes answers with his Incoherence of Incoherence. For Moslems too, the battle between God and philosophy was a fight to the death. In this instance God won, and a Moslem Nietzche might have written: 'Philosophy is dead, we all killed it together, you killed it and I killed it.'" (Ref. 4, p. 114)

After reading Paz I developed a renewed interest in studying some of the Muslim scholars. I was quite impressed when I read Pervez Hoodbhoy's book *Islam and Science*; it was an excellent postmortem of how Muslims killed scientific tradition and sacrificed it on the altar of religious orthodoxy. (Ref. 5)

While studying the history of medicine, I was fascinated to read that there was a time in the Mediaeval era when a large number of Greek writers were translated into Arabic and became accessible to the intelligentsia. The era between the 9th and the 11th century AD was considered the Golden Age of Arabic Medicine because during that period, Al-Razi (865–923), Ibn-e-Abbas and Ibn-e-Sina

(980-1037) made significant contributions to Science. Ibn-e-Sina's book *Cannon of Medicine* remained a leading textbook of medicine from the 11th to the 17th century and was widely translated into many languages. (Ref. 6)

The downfall of scientific tradition in the Muslim world is a long, sad story which is very eloquently told by Pervez Hoodbhoy, who highlights the social, economic, political and religious factors that played significant role in that decline.

> *"About 700 years ago, Islamic civilization almost completely lost the will and ability to do science. Since that time, apart from attempts during the Ottoman period and in Mohammad Ali's Egypt, there have been no significant efforts at recovery. Many Muslims acknowledge, and express profound regret at this fact. Indeed this is the major pre-occupation of the modernist faction in Islam. But most traditionalists feel no regret—in fact many welcome this loss because, in their view, keeping a distance from science helps preserve Islam from corrupting, secular influences."*
> (Ref. 5, p. 1)

Hoodbhoy has discussed the role of Ghazzali in influencing the attitudes of Muslims towards logic, rational thought and science. Ghazzali was critical of mathematics because he believed,

> *"There are two drawbacks which arise from mathematics. The first is that every student of mathematics admires its*

precision and the clarity of its demonstrations. This leads him to believe in the philosophers and to think that all their sciences resemble this one in clarity and demonstrative power. Further, he has already heard the accounts on everybody's lips of their unbelief, their denial of God's attributes, and their contempt for revealed truth: he becomes an unbeliever merely by accepting them as authorities." (Ref. 5, p. 105)

While reading Hoodbhoy's articles I was also introduced to the writings of Abdus Salam, who in the twentieth century tried to bring Religion and Science together. He did not see any conflict between his religious and scientific beliefs. He thought they belonged to two different worlds.

"I have myself never seen any dichotomy between my faith and my science, since faith was predicted for me by the timeless spiritual message of Islam, on matters on which physics is silent." (Ref. 7).

It is interesting to note that Salam and Weinberg shared a Nobel Prize by presenting the Salam-Weinberg theory,

"The fundamental theory uniting two basic forces of nature —the 'weak' and the 'electromagnetic' which according to the scientist Hoodbhoy is '...one of the most profound discoveries of this century.'" (Ref. 5)

From Islam to Secular Humanism

Salam, who was brought up in the Islamic tradition and Weinberg who was a product of Jewish culture, stood side by side in the field of Science but were worlds apart in their religious beliefs. Salam was a strong believer and Weinberg was an "atheist for whom the universe is an existentialist reality devoid of sense and purpose." (Ref. 5, p. 146) The Salam-Weinberg case clearly highlights that Science is a secular discipline with its independent traditions and standards; and the personal beliefs of scientists are irrelevant when it comes to their scientific discoveries.

As my studies progressed, I became aware that there have been a number of scientists and theologians who wanted to end the hostility between Religion and Science. They thought that the war had been between orthodox theologians and arrogant scientists. They believe that if Science and Religion defined their boundaries and respected each other's territories, then Science and Religion could become friends and even complement each other. Two such intellectuals that tried to revolutionize their respective traditions are Albert Einstein from the Scientific domain and Karen Armstrong from the Religious. Einstein through his writings tried to define boundaries between Science and Religion. He believed Science deals with WHAT IS and Religion with WHAT SHOULD BE.

"Yet it is equally clear that knowledge of what IS does not open the door directly to what SHOULD BE. One can have the clearest and most complete knowledge of what IS,

and yet not be able to deduct from that what should be the GOAL of our human aspirations." ..."For Science can only ascertain what IS, but not what SHOULD BE." (Ref. 8, p. 45)

That is why he believed that Science and Religion complemented each other. His famous quotation is,

"...science without religion is lame, religion without science is blind." (Ref. 8, p. 46)

Einstein believed that in a materialistic world when people are motivated by their greed, only those people could devote their lives to Science who were religious and spiritual in nature.

"A contemporary has said, not unjustly, that in this materialistic age of ours, the serious scientific workers are the only profoundly religious people." (Ref. 8)

While scientists like Einstein have been encouraging us to develop a spiritual attitude towards Science, similarly, theologians like Karen Armstrong, who was a nun for a number of years and then left the convent to explore the truths of other monotheistic religions, invite us to see Religion and God in a new light. She believes that in the modern world there is no room for a personal God or institutional religion. She feels that even those who believe that Traditional God was dead when Nietzche announced it at the end of the 19th century had to review their position during the Holocaust. She is very graphic, profound and perturbing when she writes,

> "One day the Gestapo hanged a child. Even the SS were disturbed by the prospect of hanging a young boy in front of thousands of spectators. The child who, Elie Weisel recalled, had the face of a 'sad-eyed angel' was silent, lividly pale and almost calm as he ascended the gallows. Behind Wiesel, one of the other prisoners asked, 'Where is God? Where is He?' It took the child half an hour to die, while the prisoners were forced to look him in the face. The same man asked again, 'Where is God now?' And Wiesel heard a voice within him make this answer: Where is He? Here He is.... He is hanging here on this gallows'...
> "Many Jews can no longer subscribe to the biblical idea of God who manifests himself in history, who, they say with Wiesel, died in Auschwitz. The idea of a personal God, like one of us writ large, is fraught with difficulty. If this God is omnipotent, he could have prevented the Holocaust. If he was unable to stop it, he is impotent and useless, if he could have stopped it and chose not to, he is a monster. Jews are not the only people who believe that the Holocaust put an end to conventional theology." (Ref. 9, p. 376)

Although disillusioned with the idea of a personal God and disappointed in institutional Religion, Armstrong is still hopeful. She suggests that we adopt the philosophy of saints and mystics and darveshes (mystic travelers) because they had a more evolved belief system, a philosophy in which God is within all of us, a belief system that transcends religious institutions, a point of view that is inclusive and could be accepted by everyone, even feminists, who were always critical of the concept of a Male God.

> "The God of the mystics might seem to present a possible alternative. The mystics have long insisted that God is not an-Other Being; they have claimed that he does not really exist and that it is better to call him Nothing. This God is in tune with the atheistic mood of our secular society, with its distrust of inadequate images of the Absolute. ...This God is to be approached through the imagination and can be seen as a kind of art form, akin to the other great artistic symbols that have expressed the ineffable mystery, beauty and value of life. Mystics have used music, dancing, poetry, fiction, stories, painting, sculpture and architecture to express this Reality that goes beyond concepts. ...The God of the mystics could even satisfy the feminists, since both Sufis and Kabbalists have long tried to introduce a female element into the divine." (Ref. 9, p. 396)

It seems as if in the twentieth century, scientists as well as theologians have been involved in soul-searching to leave their arrogance behind and adopt a more friendly, humane and spiritual attitude. It appears as though some of the religious institutions are going through a similar process and are reviewing their past traditions. Scientists all over the world were thrilled when they heard that the Catholic church which had persecuted Galileo, one of the pioneers of Science, for his discoveries that did not match the literal interpretations of the Bible, had reviewed its position towards Galileo and his work.

> "At a special ceremony in the Vatican on May 9th, 1983, the Pope declared, 'The Church's experience, during the Galileo affair and after it, has led to a more mature attitude. ...The Church herself learns by experience and reflection and she now understands better the meaning that must be given to freedom of research...one of the noblest attributes of man. It is through research that man attains the Truth. ...This is why the Church is convinced that there can be no real contradiction between science and faith... (However) it is only through humble and assiduous study that (the Church) learns to dissociate the essential of the faith from the scientific systems of a given age, especially when a culturally influenced reading of the Bible seemed to be linked to an obligatory cosmogany.'"
> (Ref. 7)

It was a three-hundred-and-fifty-year overdue apology of Religion to Science but it was better arriving late then never.

It seems as though the time has come when Science and Religion can have a friendly exchange to define their boundaries and respect each others' territories. As far as future is concerned, both disciplines, Science as well as

Religion, have new challenges to face. In the discipline of Science, Stephen Hawking writes,

> "*Today scientists describe the universe in terms of two basic partial theories...the general theory of relativity and quantum mechanics. They are great intellectual achievements of the first half of the century...*
>
> *...The eventual goal of science is to provide a single theory that describes the whole universe.*" (Ref. 10, p.10).

The challenge for Religion is to provide the moral and spiritual values that will satisfy the needs of multicultural communities and societies that have adopted the philosophy of Secular Humanism.

I hope that in the future we see an honest, sincere and candid dialogue between Science and Religion; but for such a dialogue we need to increase public education, arrange conferences and establish universities that provide a nurturing and challenging atmosphere so that a liberal attitude towards life can continue to flourish and help to bring the world into greater understanding.

References

1. Russell, Bertrand. *Why I am Not a Christian*, A Touchstone Book, New York, 1957.
2. Freud, Sigmund. *The Future of an Illusion*, W.W. Norton and Co., New York, 1961.
3. Soyinka, Wole. Art, *Dialogue and Outrage*, Panthem Books, New York, 1993.
4. Paz, Octavio. *Alternating Current*, Arcade Publishing, New York, 1967.
5. Hoodbhoy, Pervez. *Islam and Science*, Zed Books Ltd., London, 1991.
6. Jackson, Stanley. *Melancholia and Depression*, Yale University Press, 1986.
7. Salam, Abdus. "Science and Religion," Lecture Delivered at International Symposium, Cordoba, 1987.
8. Einstein, Albert. *Ideas and Opinions*, Crown Trade Paperbacks, New York, 1982.
9. Armstrong, Karen. *A History of God*, Ballantine Books, New York, 1993.
10. Hawking, Stephen. *A Brief History of Time*, Bantam Books, New York, 1990.

K. Sohail

Religion and Mysticism

Do all cultures have a religion?
Do all cultures have a concept of God and Divinity?
Do mystics from different traditions believe in the same thing?
Is mysticism a philosophy, a spiritual experience or a lifestyle?
Can someone be a mystic without believing in God and following a Religion?
Can a common man have spiritual experiences without following any mystic path?

These are some of the simple but profound questions we face when we try to understand the mysterious relationship between Religion and Mysticism.

When we study the history of different cultures and their religious and spiritual traditions, we become aware that the same words and terms are used by different scholars and lay people to reflect different ideas, concepts, philosophies and experiences. It is also evident that our understanding of different human experiences has changed over the centuries. In spite of those historical, cultural and personal differences, it is still quite fascinating to study and appreciate the similarities in how human beings, individually and collectively, all over the world, have been trying to experience, express and share the spiritual dimension of life.

There is no doubt that all communities in the world, throughout history, had a philosophy that guided their relationship with themselves, other human beings and with nature but whether they can be called Religions is a question open to interpretation.

Without getting into an academic debate, we can comfortably say that when we discuss Religion in our day-to-day lives we associate the concepts of a personal God, a Creator, prophets, scriptures, morality, places to worship like churches, synagogues, temples and mosques, religious leaders like priests, rabbis and maulanas, Life after Death, Day of Judgement and Heaven and Hell with the concept of Religion and consider Judaism, Christianity and Islam as some of the major religions of the world.

According to this traditional concept Buddhism, Jainism and Communism, because they do not believe in God, will not be considered Religions.

"Like the Buddhists," Parrinder writes, *"the Jains do not believe in an eternal creator God."* (Ref. 1, p. 49)

But if every organized life philosophy can be included under the umbrella of Religion then Buddhism and Communism can also be considered Religions, although many Buddhists and Communists may be offended to see their philosophy categorized as Religion. Parrinder continues,

> "...some have therefore maintained that Buddhism began as a philosophy or ethic and degenerated into a religion."
> (Ref. 1, p. 54)

Many of them even believe that one of the goals of their philosophy was to highlight the institutionalized aspect of Religion and free people from its negative effects.

> Religion was called "the opiate of the masses" by Karl Marx. (Ref. 1, p. 22)

Alongside the institutional aspect, many followers of Religion believe that there is another aspect of Religion that is personal and spiritual and transcends the institutional aspect of Religion. Those people that follow the path seriously are known as mystics. They have a keen interest in directly experiencing the Truth, the Reality, the Divinity and getting in touch with God rather than just understanding it intellectually. They prefer experience over knowledge. Such people like to meditate and contemplate the mysteries of the universe.

> "The origins of the word mysticism were in the Mysteries of ancient Greece. This name was perhaps derived from muein, to close the lips or eyes, with the probably primary sense of 'one vowed to keep silence' and hence 'one initiated into the Mysteries.'" (Ref. 1, p. 8)

I.M. Lewis believed that a spiritual dimension was present in all religions and the desire to get in touch with divinity was present in all cultures.

"It is difficult to find a religion which had not, at some stage in its history, inspired in the breasts of at least certain of its followers those transports of mystical exaltation in which man's whole being seems to fuse in a glorious communion with the divinity." (Ref. 2, p. 18)

Those people who chose the path of mysticism are called mystics, saints, sants, sadhus, darveshes and sufis depending on which tradition they belong to.

"I define the word sufi in wide terms," Trimingham states, *"by applying it to anyone who believes that it is possible to have direct experience of God and who is prepared to go out of his way to put himself in a state whereby he may be enabled to do this."* (Ref. 3, p. 1)

When we study lives of different mystics and the traditions they have followed over the centuries we come to know that in spite of personal and cultural differences they can be broadly classified into three groups:

1. Theistic Mysticism
2. Monistic Mysticism
3. Secular Mysticism

The first group of mystics who believe in Theistic Mysticism believe in a Creator, a God that exists outside and separate from human beings and the goal of mystic experience is to UNITE with that Being. This desire to UNITE is inspired by love and culminates in an experience where humanity touches the divinity. Such holy UNITY is the dream of those mystics. Many mystics from Monotheistic Religions like Judaism, Christianity and Islam belong to this group. There are some mystics from the Hindu Religion who also believe in One God and belong to the same group.

The second group of mystics from the Monistic tradition believe that "All That Exists is God" so they do not aspire for UNION, they rather hope for IDENTITY. Their mystic experiences make them aware that they are part of a Bigger, Higher, Deeper Reality named God and they are part of it. Many Hindu mystics, some Shinto mystics and some Muslim Sufis belong to that tradition.

The third group of mystics from the Secular tradition do not believe in a Theistic or a Monistic God, but they still look forward to a special relationship with themselves or nature that is spiritual. They believe that Life has a spiritual dimension but that spiritual dimension has no relationship to God or any organized or institutional Religion. Such Secular Mysticism can be:

Nature Mysticism—if the experience is through Nature or, *Self Mysticism*—when the goal is to get in touch with deeper and higher aspect of one's Self. Such mystics believe that all human beings alongside a materialistic dimension, also have a spiritual dimension and getting in touch with that dimension makes us better human beings.

Many followers of Buddha in India, Confucius in China, Shinto in Japan and Secular Humanism in the West and East belong to that group.

For many people the differences between these groups might be academic, but mystics belonging to different groups have strong feelings and reactions to the other groups. For example, these followers of Hindu tradition who believe in one God and Theistic Mysticism are very critical of those Hindus who believe in Monistic Mysticism. Devendranath Tagore (1818-1905) expressed these feelings about Sankara and his Monistic interpretation of the Upanishads

> *"Shankaracharya has turned India's head by preaching the doctrine of Monism, the identity of God and man. Following his teachings, both ascetics and men of the world are repeating this senseless formula "I am that Supreme Deity."* (Ref. 4, p. 199)

Similarly those Muslim Sufis who believe in Monism were criticized by Theistic mystics and accused of heresy and even persecuted. One such example was Ibn Arabi. When Ibn Arabi expressed his Monistic beliefs in these words, he was attacked for heresy:

> *"When the mystery...of realizing that the mystic is one with the Divine...is revealed to you, you will have the*

understanding that you are not, other than God ... You will see all your actions to be his actions and all your attributes to be his attributes and your essence to be his essence." (Ref. 5, p. 83)

There are also different views on Secular mystics. For example, "Nature mystics have been attacked in the assumption that identification with nature is the same as union with God" (Ref. 1, P. 25), although Nature mystics, themselves, do not associate Nature with God. Richard Jefferies who held that "there is no God in nature" may be classed among those who "sought communion with earth and sky but felt no more." (Ref. 1, p. 28) Similarly many other Secular mystics want only to get in touch with their own deeper and higher selves and see spirituality as part of humanity and do not associate it with divinity.

The question arises: "What are the characteristics of that world that mystics call a spiritual world?" When we read the biographies and philosophies of different mystics, we become aware that many of them have described that world in the terms of "What It Is Not" rather than "What It Is." They consider it a world that is nameless, formless, timeless and pathless.

"No miseries befall one who does not cling to name and form."
Buddha (Ref. 6)

"Sufi-ism is truth without form." Ibn-e-Jalali (Ref. 7)

"Pass from time and place to timelessness and placelessness, to other worlds. There is our origin." Smarquandi Amini (Ref. 7)

"Truth is a pathless land." Krishnamurti (Ref. 8)

Mystics from different traditions are aware that common people live in a materialistic world, a world that exists in time and space and use words, forms and names to identify and share their observations and experiences; but those names and forms conceal more than they reveal and get in touch with only a part of the Reality. They see only the tip of the iceberg. Mystics encounter the Reality that is beyond the obvious, that is beyond our natural senses, but then they find it difficult to share their spiritual experiences and mystical encounters. They ask themselves:

How do we talk about a world where sounds turn mute?
How do we talk about a world where words lose all their meanings?
How do we discuss a world that transcends every logic?
How do we describe a world that has no boundaries?
How do we conceptualize a world that defies any form?
How do we understand a world that is beyond words and sounds and colours and space and time and logic and...?

Since it has been very difficult to talk about the spiritual world in a rational way and share mystical experiences in a logical way, many mystics adopted a symbolic and metaphorical form of expression. Armstrong wrote,

"Mystics have used music, dancing, poetry, fiction, stories, painting, sculpture and architecture to express this Reality that goes beyond concepts..." (Ref. 9, p. 396)

When we see the paintings of William Blake and read poetry by Wordsworth, Whitman, Hafiz, Rumi, Baba Farid, Kabir Das and other mystic poets from different spiritual traditions, we have a few glimpses of that mysterious world.

It is interesting to read how many mystics chose to walk on the mystic path and travelled a spiritual journey in order to get in touch with the spiritual world and to have mystical experiences. Different traditions of Mysticism have suggested different paths. Some of them are life-denying while others are life-affirming. Many mystics belonging to Hindu and Christian Mysticism have adopted the life-denying path, left their families and jobs and gone to jungles and monasteries hundreds of miles away from their communities. For years, sometimes decades, they deprived themselves of all kinds of worldly pleasures hoping that such a sacrifice would purify them and help them achieve spiritual enlightenment. It is interesting to note that some of those mystics remained in jungles and monasteries for the rest of their lives, while others, after achieving spiritual enlightenment, came back to the community to share their experiences and wisdom, helping others to adopt a saintly lifestyle. Their compassion for others overcame their isolation. Buddha, after achieving Nirvana, spent years teaching, helping and serving people.

> "A cardinal Mahayana doctrine is that of Bodhi-sattva, the 'enlightened-being', or one whose 'essence is enlightenment'. This is one who has progressed far on the path and is on the brink of Nirvana, but then refuses to enter it until all other creatures are saved. This is a doctrine of compassion, in which love has replaced Nirvana as the ideal... For Mahayana the idea of compassion was illustrated by Buddha himself, who combined both the self-denial which led to enlightenment, and the life of service that followed. Instead of proceeding to Nirvana, he spent forty years in compassion to mankind..." (Ref. 1, p. 64)

Buddha highlighted that spiritual enlightenment and compassion for other human beings are two aspects of Mysticism and are very intimately connected and necessary for our personal and social growth.

When we study the biographies of mystics from a psychological point of view, we are struck by their unique personalities and lifestyles. Through following the spiritual path, hard work and discipline, they develop some of the following characteristics.

1. Contentment

Mystics acquire a sense of contentment in their lives. They become aware that one of the reasons ordinary people do not have peace of mind is that they are greedy. Most people live with an illusion that material things, whether they are dollars, houses, cars, boats or other luxurious things in life, can make them happy. They do not realize that greediness is a self-feeding process. Mystics believe that the world is like an ocean and the human heart a boat. As long as the water stays outside, the boat is safe; but when the boat starts to leak and water comes in, then two gallons of water is more dangerous than tons of water in the ocean. Mystics even when surrounded by beautiful, expensive and luxurious things are not emotionally attached to them. They use them only for pragmatic reasons. That is why they don't feel excited if they gain a lot nor do they get depressed if they lose materialistic possessions. They know that their spiritual growth is more significant than physical belongings. They are aware that all human beings enter and leave this world empty-handed and that is why they do not really own anything. They know that alongside their houses and cars, their children and even their own lives are temporary possessions. They are just the caretakers. They know that most people live with an illusion of owning their houses and spouses and children and get depressed when they lose them one day.

"I have sons. I have wealth. The fool suffers thinking thus. Even one's self is not one's own; how then sons, how then wealth?" Buddha (Ref. 6)

"And a woman who held a babe against her bosom said, Speak to us of children.

From Islam to Secular Humanism

> *And he said: Your children are not your children.*
> *They are the sons and daughters of Life's longing for itself.*
> *They come through you but not from you.*
> *And though they are with you, yet they belong not to you.*
> *You may give them your love but not your thoughts.*
> *For they have their own thoughts.*
> *You may house their bodies but not their souls.*
> *For their souls dwell in the house of tomorrow, which you cannot visit, not even in your dreams... "*
>
> Khalil Gibran (Ref. 10)

Many mystics have renounced their materialistic possessions before joining the spiritual journey. One such example was a Muslim mystic Abraham-bin-adham who was a king before he became a mystic. According to the legend, one night when he was sleeping in his palace he heard someone walking on the roof. He called out,

"What are you searching for on the roof?"

"My lost camel."

"How can you find a camel on the roof?" he laughed.

"The same way you are looking for God in the palace." The next day Ibrahim-bin-adham left the palace and followed a path to the jungle.

2. Humility

Mystics are humble people. They are more concerned about people's characters than their background, social class or worldly possessions. They realize that all human beings are born equal and the only people who deserve more respect and reverence are those who have worked hard to grow spiritually. Mystics are indifferent to worldly hierarchies and divisions of people based on religious, linguistic, class and other differences. Mystics respect and accept common people and their innocence rather than judging them.

In mystic literature there is a story of a vazir who used to visit a special room before going to his bedroom every night. Nobody knew what was in that room. On his deathbed the vazir shared his secret that he was a very poor man before he became a vazir and he had kept his rags in that room so that they could remind him of his humble beginnings before he went to sleep every night. The whole nation benefited from the vazir's humility and wisdom as long as he served his people.

A raindrop, dripping from a cloud,
Was ashamed when it saw the sea.
Who am I where there is a sea? it said
When it saw itself with the eye of humility,
A shell nurtured it in its embrace.

Saadi Shirazi (Ref. 7)

Mystics are aware that the biggest hurdle in their spiritual journey is their own SELF. It is the selfish self-love that makes it difficult for people to make the sacrifices necessary to succeed in spiritual growth.

Farid-ud-din Attar wrote:

The self has swallowed you for its delight
How long will you endure its mindless spite?
Abandon such self-love and you will see
The Way that leads us to Reality. (Ref. 15)

3. Beyond Reward and Punishment

Most people are like children, motivated by the principles of reward and punishment. They want instantaneous gratification. They like to see concrete results of their efforts.

Those who are more mature, are able to sacrifice their short term rewards for long term gains. Some even make sacrifices all their lives hoping to go to heaven after they die.

Mystics are those evolved human beings who can transcend the concepts of heaven and hell. For them virtue is its own reward. Even those mystics who believe in God serve others and pray out of love, not duty.

"O Lord!
If I worship you from fear of hell, cast me into hell.
If I worship you from desire for paradise, deny me
paradise." Rabia Basri (Ref. 7)

4. Inner Peace and Harmony

Mystics do what feels natural to them and gradually achieve inner peace and harmony. They are aware that they cannot change the whole world but they can change their own world by following the trail of their own hearts rather than following the highway of tradition. As they progress on the spiritual path they develop a consistency and harmony in their feeling and thoughts and words and actions. Because of such a consistency they also do not experience feelings of guilt and remorse. It comes natural to them to dissolve and resolve conflicts and accept situations they cannot change. Because they are quite peaceful in their own life, people who are in their company also share that peace. They radiate tranquility.

Buddha said, "If one speaks or acts with a pure mind, happiness will follow, like a shadow that never leaves." (Ref. 6)

5. Healers

Mystics adopt a lifestyle of healers rather than preachers. They practise what they believe in and share their care with whomever they come across.

Mystics have always been compassionate to common people. Their doors and hearts are always open to people from all walks of life. They try to help the needy and the poor and offer support to the sick and disabled. It is not uncommon to see mystics working as nurses and doctors and voluntary workers in clinics and hospitals offering their services whenever communities need them.

Mother Teresa was an excellent example of a mystic who selflessly served the poor and the sick for half a century.

Walt Whitman, a mystic poet, offered his services to

the Soldier's Hospital in Washington during the Civil War. One of his friends wrote about one of his visits to the hospital in these words, "Never shall I forget that visit...to one he gave a few words of cheer, for another he wrote a letter home, to others he gave an orange, a few comfits [sugar confection], a cigar, a pipe and tobacco, a sheet of paper or a postage stamp, all of which and many other things were in his capacious haversack...he did the things for them which no nurse or doctor could do, and he seemed to leave a benediction at every cot as he passed along... He performed miracles, the doctors said,... miracles of healing." (Ref. 12)

Many of the soldiers remembered him years later as "the man with the face of a Saviour." Walt Whitman wrote a beautiful poem describing his feelings at the sight of a slain enemy.

> "Word over all, beautiful as the sky,
> Beautiful that war and all its carnage must in time be utterly lost,
> That the hands of the sisters death and night incessantly softly wash again, and ever again, this soil'd world;
> For my enemy is dead, a man divine as myself is dead;
> I look where he lies white-faced and stiff in the coffin
>   ...I draw near,
> Bend down and touch lightly with my lips the white face in the coffin." (Ref. 12)

K. Sohail

Mystics have a humanistic attitude. They can see a human being even in their enemy.

6. Accepting Death Gracefully

Mystics are not afraid of death. They see it as another step in the journey rather than the end of the journey. They accept death gracefully rather than resentfully. Because they live peacefully they are ready to die peacefully.

Tagore wrote:

> *"On the day when death will knock at thy door what will thou offer him?*
> *Oh, I will set before my guest the full vessel of my life.*
> *I will never let him go with empty hands.*
> *All the sweet vintage of all my autumn days and summer nights,*
> *all the earnings and gleanings of my busy life will I place before him*
> *at the close of my days when death will knock on my door."*
> (Ref. 13)

Kabir Das said:

> *"O brother*
> *all that is born*
> *must die*
> *that is the law of nature*
> *the fool believes it to be*

> *the end of the journey*
> *the wise men knows*
> *it is only a step*
> *in the journey."* (Ref. 11)

Mystics know that the search for truths does not end with death. Such a search has been going on for centuries and will continue till the last human being in the universe.

7. Role in Human Evolution

Mystics throughout the world over the centuries have played a significant role in human evolution. They helped people to get in touch with their own truth and discover divinity in the depths of their souls. On one hand they were role models for spiritual enlightenment and on the other hand paved the way for compassionate life. Mystics were sought out by people not only when they were alive but also as a source of inspiration even after their deaths.

Jala-uddin-Rumi said:

> *"When we are dead,*
> *seek not our tomb in the earth*
> *but find it*
> *in the hearts of men."* (Ref. 7)

8. Beyond Institutions

Mystics follow their own hearts and encourage others to do the same. That is why they are perceived as a threat by social, political and religious institutions.

K. Sohail

Kabir Das said:

"O Brahman
I say only
What I have seen
With my own eyes
And you keep quoting
The scriptures
I speak
To unravel
The mystery
But you insist
On keeping it
Tangled
How can our paths
Cross?" (Ref. 11)

Since mystics were critical of blind faith and adherence to religious traditions without exploring one's personal truth, many of them were punished, persecuted, and even killed by traditional religious people and organizations. There have been many such examples over the centuries. One famous example is of a Mystic Mansoor Hallaj.

"...Hallaj seems to have taken the doctrine of unity to extremes by declaring 'I am the real' (AnulHuq) or 'the Creative Truth' which was regarded as blasphemy, since these were attributes of God alone. Hallaj was tortured *and executed in Baghdad in 922, but he has been one of the most discussed Sufis ever since..."*

Like many other Sufis, Hallaj stressed the love of God, and it was this love which led him to feel a unity with God, expressed in one of his most famous verses:

"I have become he whom I love, and he has become myself, We are two spirits in one body, When you see me you see him." (Ref. 1, p. 135)

In the twentieth century, as the frontiers of science and human psychology expanded, many scientists and psychologists started studying the spiritual dimension of the human personality. As their research grew they brought to our awareness that spirituality did not belong only in churches, monasteries and jungles, it could be part of our day to day life. They highlighted that spiritual experiences were not restricted only to mystics, rather, they were an integral part of our day to day life. Psychologists like Abraham Maslow are trying to study spirituality as part of human nature. They want to come up with observations, findings and conclusions that "can be accepted as real by clergymen and atheists alike." (Ref. 14, p. 54)

Maslow was of the opinion that segregation of sacred and profane, saint and sinner, mystic and pragmatist is artificial and unnatural. He tried to reclaim spirituality as part of our humanity.

K. Sohail

"I want to demonstrate that spiritual values have naturalistic meaning, that they are not the exclusive possession of organized churches, that they do not need supernatural concepts to validate them, that they are within the jurisdiction of a suitably enlarged science, and that, therefore, they are the general responsibility of all mankind."
(Ref. 14, p.4)

Maslow believed that ordinary men and women can have extraordinary experiences, and unusual things can happen in usual circumstances. Maslow named those special experiences "peak experiences." He described a number of characteristics of these experiences that can occur spontaneously in the life of any layperson, poet, intellectual, scientist, artist or religious person while watching a sunset, playing with one's grandchild, making love, composing a poem or contemplating the mysteries of the universe, although certain types of practices and disciplines might make the likelihood of these experiences more probable and more frequent. He believed that those human experiences are called spiritual/religious/mystic because of the belief system of that individual, community and culture. By calling them peak experiences and highlighting that a religious belief was not a prerequisite to have them, Maslow tried to secularize the spiritual and religious world. Without going into a detailed discussion of peak experiences I will just share a couple of characteristics:

> "...it is quite characteristic of peak experiences that the whole universe is perceived as an integrated and unified whole. This is not as simple a happening as one might imagine from the bare words themselves. To have a clear perception (rather than a purely abstract and verbal philosophical acceptance) that the universe is all of a piece and that one has his place in it...one is a part of it, one belongs to it...can be so profound and shaking an experience that it can change the person's character..."
>
> "...in a peak experience such emotions as wonder, awe, reverence, humility, surrender and even worship before the greatness of the experience are often reported." (Ref. 14, p. 59, 65)

Maslow also studied the changes in people's personalities after they had had those special peak experiences. He observed that in some people those experiences had a profound impact on people's personalities and lifestyles.

> "...the peak experiencer becomes more loving and more accepting, and so he becomes more spontaneous and honest and innocent."
>
> "...people during and after peak experiences characteristically feel lucky, fortunate, graced. A common reaction is, "I don't deserve this." (Ref. 14, p. 76)

Maslow even wonders whether leaving one's day-to-day life with one's family, friends, colleagues and neighbours, not being involved in one's community and going to jungles and monasteries in search of Nirvana may even be a reflection of escaping from one's realities and social responsibilities. It might also reflect that one does not believe that everything in life is sacred and has the potential to be miraculous.

> *"The search for the exotic, the strange, the unusual, the uncommon has often taken the form of pilgrimages, of turning away from the world, the 'Journey to the East' to another country or to a different religion. The great lesson from the true mystics, from the Zen monks, and now also from the Humanistic and Transpersonal psychologists... that the sacred is in the ordinary, that it is to be found in one's daily life, in one's neighbours, friends and family, in one's backyard, and that travel may be a flight from confronting the sacred...this lesson can be easily lost. To be looking elsewhere for miracles is to me a sign of ignorance that everything is miraculous."* (Ref. 14, p. X)

The idea that the whole universe is sacred is quite well developed in Native Indian spiritual tradition, a tradition, that has been fully acknowledged and appreciated neither in the West nor in the East over the centuries.

When we read the writings of Chief Seattle, Black Elk and other Native Indian wise men and women, we become aware that in their worldview, human beings, animals and birds are considered part of the same family. They believe that whether they are rivers or mountains, the suns or the moons, the deserts or the galaxies, all are part of a cosmos that is holy and we as human beings are spiritually connected to them.

Peter Blue Cloud Mohawk:

"Will you ever begin to understand the meaning of the very soil beneath your feet?
From a grain of sand to a great mountain, all is sacred. We natives are guardians of this sacred place." (Ref. 16)

Zuni saying:

"The landscape is our church, a cathedral. It is like a sacred building to us." (Ref. 16)

Chief Seattle:

"Every part of this country is sacred to my people." (Ref. 17)

Tagore, the Eastern mystic poet, believed that getting in touch with one's true self is the ultimate goal of spiritual growth:

"The traveler has to knock at every alien door
to come to his own,
and one has to wander through all the outer worlds
to reach the innermost shrine at the end." Tagore (Ref. 13)

Sahil of Qazwin taught his disciples, "Whoever knocks at the door continually, it will open to him."

K. Sohail

Rabia Basri hearing him one day said, "How long will you say 'It will be opened?' The door has never been shut."
(Ref. 7)

References

1. Parrinder, Geoffery. *Mysticism in The World's Religions*, Oneworld, Oxford, 1976.
2. Lewis, I.M. *Ecstatic Religion*, England, 1971.
3. Trimingham, J.S. *The Sufi Orders In Islam*, USA, 1971.
4. Tagore, M.D. *The Autobiography of Maharishi Devendranath Tagore*, USA, 1915.
5. Landau, R. *The Philosophy of Ibn Arabi*, England, 1959.
6. Buddha. *Dhammapada*, Translation by Thomas Cleary, Bantam Books, USA, 1995.
7. Idries, Shah. *The Way of the Sufi*, Penguin Books, England, 1968.
8. White, John, Editor. *What Is Enlightenment?*, Jeremy Tarcher Inc. USA, 1984.
9. Armstrong, Karen. *A History of God*, Ballantine Books, USA, 1993.
10. Gibran, Kahlil. *The Prophet*, Jarco Publishing House, USA, 1957.
11. Kumar, Sehdev. *The Vision of Kabir*, Alpha and Omega Books, Canada, 1984.
12. Henry, Thomas and Lees, Dana. *Living Biographies of Great Poets*, Garden City Books, USA, 1984.
13. Tagore, Rabindranath. *Gitanjali*, MacMillan Publishers Ltd., England, 1913.
14. Maslow, Abraham. *Religions, Values and Peak Experiences*, Penguin Books, England, 1970.
15. Attar, Farid-ud-din, *The Conference of the Birds*, Penguin Books, England, 1984.
16. Reiger, Willis, Editor, *Masterpieces of American Indian Literature*, MJF Books New York, 1993.
17. Cassidy, James Editor, *Through Indian Eyes: The Untold Story of Native Peoples*, Readers Digest Association Canada, 1996.

From Islam to Secular Humanism

Siddhartha

A Symbol of Spiritual Journey

Of all the books I have read about enlightenment, the one that is closest to my heart is *Siddhartha*, a novel by Hermann Hesse. It is a fictionalized version of Buddha's story. In this novel all the colours of the rainbow of spirituality and creativity have come together as a bright light. I have read the novel numerous times and each time I discover new insights into the human condition. Hermann Hesse has captured the essence of Buddha's life in one hundred pages. Each page depicts a step of the spiritual journey—a journey towards the mysteries of life, a journey towards the borders of divinity, a journey towards the depths of one's soul, a journey that is common to all mystics, all Siddharthas who wait to become Buddhas.

In history books when we study the legend of Buddha who has remained a symbol of enlightenment for centuries, we come to know that he was a prince of India in about 500 B.C. and was raised in an overprotective environment by his rich father. He was never let out of the palace because astronomers had made predictions that if he was exposed to certain aspects of the human condition he might leave the palace and choose to be a mystic rather than a king. Although his father tried his best to prevent that fate because he wanted to hand over his dynasty to his son and wanted him to rule the kingdom, according to the myth he did not succeed. Buddha one day went through the northern gate of the palace to visit the city. On his way back he saw a man sitting on the roadside crying. His features were distorted and his limbs crippled. He asked his servants what was wrong with him. They told him that he was a leper. The second week he went through the southern gate and saw a man whose back was bent over and was walking with a stick. On asking his servants he was told that he was an old man and all of us one day will become like him. The third week he went through the eastern gate and saw a human body lying motionless on the cot and people were preparing a fire. On inquiring he found out that the person was dead and he was going to be cremated. The fourth week when Buddha went through the western gate he saw a half-naked man walking in the street talking to himself, oblivious to his environment. When Buddha asked his companions, he was told that the man was a saint and had discarded the luxuries of life. After having encounters with illness, old age, death and mysticism the astrologers' prediction came true and he decided to leave home to find himself. Buddha's father was quite disappointed to see his son leave the palace. Hermann Hesse in his novel beautifully paints the conflict between the son and his father.

K. Sohail

"Siddhartha said, 'With your permission, Father, I have to tell you that I wish to leave your house tomorrow and join the ascetics. I wish to become a Samana. I trust my father will not object.' ...Then his father said, 'It is not seemly for Brahmins to utter forceful and angry words, but there is displeasure in my heart. I should not like to hear you make this request a second time.'"

After that exchange the father left the room but Siddhartha stood there pensive and motionless. He had already decided what his next step was going to be. He just did not want to be disrespectful to his father. When his father woke up in the middle of the night and looked outside his bedroom window he saw Siddhartha standing in the same position in which he had left him hours ago. Throughout the night whenever he woke up he saw his son standing there motionless. By the morning the father knew very well that his son was determined to pursue his spiritual journey.

"The first light of day entered the room. The Brahmin saw that Siddhartha's knees trembled slightly, but there was no trembling in Siddhartha's face; his eyes looked far away. Then the father realized that Siddhartha could no longer remain with him at home—that he had already left him."

It was not uncommon for mystics to leave their homes and families and properties behind, to withdraw from all worldly commitments and obligations, to go to jungles and caves and mountains and valleys close to nature away from the hypocritical world, to meditate and contemplate the nature of man and his relationship with other human beings and the universe. It was also common for their families and friends to resist and resent their departure as they felt rejected and abandoned. Sacrificing whatever they had was the first investment in their spiritual growth.

After leaving the luxuries of the materialistic world and the temptations of carnal desires, mystics go through a stringent regimen to control their bodies and minds. There is a long process of self-negation and self-annihilation and self-deprivation depending upon the tradition mystics follow. Many do not eat or talk for weeks. Others torture their bodies for months and years. They try to detach themselves from every pain and pleasure.

> *"Siddhartha had one single goal—to become empty, to become empty of thirst, desire, dreams, pleasure and sorrow—to let the Self die. No longer to be Self, to experience the peace of an emptied heart, to experience pure thought—that was his goal. When all the Self was conquered and dead, when all passions and desires were silent, then the last must awaken, the innermost of Being that is no longer Self—the great secret!"*

Finally they reach a stage where they lose their self, their ego, their pride and their narcissism and when they empty the vessel of their being completely, they are ready to receive the gift of truth, reality and light, bringing them a peace of mind, tranquillity of heart and harmony with others. That is the stage where they experience being in touch with world spirit and cosmic consciousness which they find hard to describe. Sometimes it takes them years or decades to acquire that purity of being.

Hesse writes about Siddhartha's best friend Govinda who had joined him in his spiritual journey, "Govinda murmured a verse to himself, a verse from one of the Upanishads:

'He whose reflective pure spirit sinks into Atman knows bliss inexpressible through words.'

Siddhartha was silent. He dwelt long on the words which Govinda had uttered."

After acquiring that state of mind and being, some mystics stay in the jungles or convents or khaniqahs, the mystic training centres; while others come back to the materialistic world and work and live with other human beings; but this time the living is different than the living before. They are part and not part of the greedy and exploitative and aggressive world. They are like a lotus flower that is in touch with the mud but still rises above it. When they face anger and violence and greed they rise above it and their presence becomes a strong force to bring peace to people's hearts and harmony in their relationship with their environment.

Being human beings they are tempted by their carnal

desires and even give into them from time to time but then regain their control. They realize that living with others and being tempted and struggling to resist or overcome those temptations is better than leading an isolated life in an environment where there are no temptations.

When Siddhartha came back to society he fell in love with a woman, had a child and got involved in a business hoping that he could keep a balance between his materialistic and spiritual lives; but when he realized that his spiritual journey was being undermined by his lifestyle he disappeared one night and never came back again. He met a ferryman who taught him more secrets of life, human relationships and nature. Siddhartha realized that if the quest is genuine one cannot stay at one place in the spiritual journey for very long.

While going through different stages of this journey mystics develop a spiritual personality. They develop a new relationship with themselves and people around them. When Kamala asked Siddhartha what he had learnt in his spiritual journey so far he said, "I can think, I can fast, I can wait."

And when the businessman Kamaswami challenged him by saying, "Is that all?"

"I think that is all," he replied.

"And what use are they? For example, fasting, what good is that?"

"It is of great value, sir. If a man has nothing to eat, fasting is the most intelligent thing he can do. If, for instance, Siddhartha had not learnt to fast, he would have had to seek some kind of work today, either with you, or elsewhere, for hunger would have driven him. But as it is, Siddhartha can wait calmly. He is not impatient, he is not indeed, he can ward off hunger for a long time and laugh at it. Therefore, fasting is useful, sir."

Mystics also develop a special relationship with time and space. Hesse highlights it by the dialogue between Siddhartha and his friend the ferryman Vesudeva.

"He once asked him, 'Have you also learned that secret from the river; that there is no such thing as time?'

A bright smile spread over Vesudeva's face.

'Yes, Siddhartha,' he said. 'Is that what you mean? That the river is everywhere at the same time, at the source and at the mouth, at the waterfall, at the ferry, at the current, in the ocean and in the mountains, everywhere, and that the present only exists for it, not the shadow of the past, nor the shadow of the future.'"

When saints, sufis and mystics finally achieve spiritual enlightenment, they experience a new relationship with themselves and the world and can see a unity in diversity. For them a stone, a flower, an animal, a human being and God have something in common that most people don't realize.

For them the whole universe becomes sacred.

Hesse wrote, "Siddhartha bent down, lifted a stone from the ground and held it in his hand.

'This,' he said, handling it, 'is a stone, and within a certain length of time it will perhaps be soil and from the soil it will become plant, animal or man. Previously I should have said: This stone is just a stone; it has no value, it belongs to the world of Maya, but perhaps because within the cycle of change it can also become man and spirit, it is also of importance. That is what I should have thought. But now I think: This stone is stone; it is also animal, God and Buddha. I do not respect and love it because it was one thing and will become something else, but because it has already long been everything and always is everything.'"

After finding enlightenment Buddha like many other saints and mystics and sufis spent the rest of his life teaching others to follow their hearts, transcend their religious doctrines and discover Nirvana for themselves.

It is a fascinating aspect of human history that many mystics and saints from different traditions in different parts of the world were never identified in their lives because they did not want to be in the public eye. They lived their lives quietly without worrying about punishments and rewards. They were aware that they were part of a caravan that has been playing a role in human evolution for centuries. They knew their spiritual powers and did not find a need to boast about them. They knew that they had been enriching people's lives throughout history and playing a significant role in the spiritual evolution of mankind. They had been helping people from all walks of life to discover unity in diversity and struggling against those social, political and religious institutions that have been dividing people in the name of language, class, ethnicity, race or other man-made divisions rather than bringing them together. Instead of an atmosphere of conflict and confrontation they had been creating an atmosphere of cooperation and peace and harmony. Even after their deaths those mystics and saints and sufis live in the hearts of people for centuries and their wisdom is passed on from generation to generation.

Hermann Hesse's novel *Siddhartha* is a masterpiece. It is classic and contemporary at the same time. It depicts the individuality and universality of Buddha's life in such a creative way that it becomes a symbol of a spiritual journey.

References

1. Hesse, Hermann. *Siddhartha*, New Directions Publishers, New York, 1951.

Krishnamurti

A Symbol of Freedom

Krishnamurti, a modern mystic, well known for his saying, "Truth is a pathless land," was a living legend of the twentieth century. He was a great influence on quite a few great minds of East and West in his lifetime and equally popular in all classes and strata of life. On one hand, famous politicians, scientists, artists and mystics found him a source of inspiration, and on the other, people from all walks of life came to listen to his lectures to gain wisdom and develop insights into their lives. Those who consulted him for their problems included three generations of prime ministers of India: Jawaharlal Nehru, his daughter Indira Gandhi and her son Rajiv Gandhi. People who admired his knowledge, experience and wisdom included Dalai Lama, Bernard Shaw, Aldous Huxley, Henry Miller, R.D. Laing, Joseph Campbell and many more.

Krishnamurti's life from childhood to old age had been a fascinating phenomenon. Life made special preparations to groom him for his role as a modern Buddha and Messiah. Even in his lifetime he had become a symbol of freedom and spiritual transformation, an influence that has been growing since his death.

Studying his biography, it becomes clear that he faced tremendous obstacles and unusual circumstances from his childhood. When Krishnamurti was in school he had no interest in formal education. He spent a lot of time daydreaming, communing with nature and contemplating the mysteries of life. Teachers failed to appreciate his creative personality and attached a scornful label to him. Pupul Jayakar, his biographer wrote, "Krishnamurti took little interest in the school and academic work, but spent long hours looking at the clouds, at bees, at ants and insects, and gazing into the vast distance. He has been described as sickly and mentally undeveloped. His vagueness, few words, lack of interest in worldly affairs, and eyes that gazed out at the world, seeing beyond horizons, were mistaken by his teachers for mental retardation."

Krishnamurti was quite attached to his mother as a child and on her death when he was only ten, Krishnamurti was devastated. Unfortunately his father was so busy in his work that he did not spend much time with his children, causing them to feel quite abandoned. Later, Krishnamurti revealed in his autobiography, "My mother's death in 1905 deprived my brothers and myself of the one who loved and cared for us most, and my father was too much occupied with his business to pay much attention to us.... After my mother's death, matters were worse, for there was really nobody to look after us."

While Krishnamurti was recovering from his mother's death, he came to the attention of members of The

Theosophical Society in India as they detected a spiritual aura surrounding him. In those days The Theosophical Society, which was based on the principles of Universal brotherhood and Buddhist and Hindu spiritualism, was presided over by Annie Besant and guided by Charles Leadbeater, a clergyman well known for his powers of clairvoyance. At Leadbeater's suggestion, Krishnamurti and his brother Nitya were invited to the grandiose residence of The Theosophical Society. During one of the clairvoyant investigations an Englishman became in touch with the previous incarnations of Krishnamurti and saw him as a fountain of compassion and wisdom, a disciple of Buddha. After admission to The Theosophical Society, Krishnamurti and Nitya were under strict supervision and rigorous training. They were taught in English and not allowed to speak in their mother tongue, Telugu. When Mrs. Besant met Krishnamurti in November 1909, she was so impressed that she took him under her care like a mother and within no time saw him accepted into the Esoteric Section of the Theosophical Society to nurture and train for his future role.

After entering the Esoteric section Krishnamurti's spiritual experiences began. He would enter trance states, have extraordinary visions and then write to Mrs. Besant, his spiritual guardian. In one of the letters he shared his mystical and mysterious experience with her in these words,

"When I left my body the first night, I went at once to the

Master's house and I found Him there with Master Morya and the Master Djwal Kul. The Master talked to me very kindly for a long time, and told me all about the initiation, and what I should have to do."

Mrs. Besant became so overwhelmed by Krishnamurti's spiritual powers and potential that she took him and his brother, without their father's consent, to England. Even her own colleagues put pressure on her not to take that step but she was quite determined to introduce Krishnamurti to the Western world as she believed that was going to be the future Maitreya Buddha. Krishnamurti and Nitya stayed in England from 1912 to 1922. In April 1913, at the instigation of Krishnamurti's family, even the High Court of Madras ordered Mrs. Besant to bring the children back to India but she refused. During those years Krishnamurti and Nitya faced a lot of racial prejudice in England. At one time the only job a brown-skinned boy could find in an all white-staffed-and-managed hospital was to scrub floors. Mrs. Besant tried her best to get both brothers accepted to Oxford or Cambridge but the colour of their skin was a major obstacle they could not overcome. By the time they went back to India for a short visit in December 1921, they had not seen their father for nine years. Their father did not live very long after that brief visit and died three years later.

In 1922 Krishnamurti was first invited to Sydney, Australia for a Theosophical convention, where he met his old teacher Leadbeater, and later on flew to Ojai,

California. Arriving in California was a beginning of a new chapter in Krishnamurti's life. After meditating regularly his mystical experiences became the beginning of his spiritual enlightenment. Some experiences were very painful, traumatic and bizarre. Most people around Krishnamurti were unable to fully understand those experiences but were very supportive of this mysterious journey. They believed that he was experiencing the awakening of his spiritual self, generally known in the spiritual world as "Kundalini," in which the person experiences transformations of consciousness not accessible to ordinary people. One such experience Krishnamurti described to Mrs. Besant in a letter,

"The climax was reached on the 19th. I could not think, nor was I able to do anything, and I was forced by friends here to retire to bed. Then I became almost unconscious, though I was well aware of what was happening around me. I came to myself at about noon each day. On that first day while I was in that state and more conscious of the things around me, I had the first most extraordinary experience. There was a man mending the road; that man was myself; the pickaxe he held was myself; the very stone which he was breaking was a part of me; the tender blade of grass was my very being and the tree beside the man was myself. I almost could feel and think like the roadmender, and I could feel the wind passing through the tree and the little ant on the grass I could feel. The birds, the dust and the very noise were a part of me. Just then

there was a car passing by at some distance; I was the driver, the engine and the tires; as the car went further away from me, I was going away from myself. I was in everything, or rather everything was in me, inanimate and animate, the mountain, the worm and all breathing things. All day long I remained in this happy condition....I have seen the glorious and healing Light. The fountain of Truth has been revealed to me and the darkness has been dispersed. Love in all its glory has intoxicated my heart; my heart can never be closed. I have drunk at the fountain of joy and eternal Beauty. I am God-intoxicated."

For the next few months Krishnamurti continued to have these mystical experiences. During a number of those episodes he became semi-conscious and his brother and friends had to look after him so that he did not hurt himself. Many times he would fall to the floor and experience seizure-like states. On other occasions in his trance, he regressed and talked like a little boy. On one occasion he talked about the death of his mother, revealing that it had really bothered him extensively as a little boy. He recovered from those spiritual experiences and traumas a transformed man. During one episode he became convinced that he would lose his mind and remain insane.

"They know how much a body can stand. If I become a lunatic, look after me—not that I will become a lunatic. They are very careful with the body. I feel so old. Only a

bit of me is functioning. I am like an India rubber toy, which a child plays with. It is the child that gives it life."

At the end of that spiritual journey he had visions of Buddha and other Masters of the occult hierarchy. In one vision he was given the message,

"The happiness you seek is not far off; it lies in every common stone."

After those experiences Krishnamurti started a new life. But he had not gone very far in it when his brother died and he was overwhelmed by grief. His brother was not just his brother; he was also his best friend who had gone with him through bad times and good. Krishnamurti identified with him so much that when he finally recovered from grieving he said, "Now, I know, now we are inseparable. He and I will work together, for I and my brother are one."

Gradually Krishnamurti became aware of his role in life. In February 1927 he wrote to Leadbeater,

"I know my destiny and my work. I know with certainty that I am blending into the consciousness of the one Teacher and that he will completely fill me. I feel and I know also that my cup is nearly full to the brim and that it will overflow soon. Till then I must abide quietly and with eager patience. I long to make and will make everybody happy."

From Islam to Secular Humanism

In April 1927, Mrs. Besant said to the Associated Press in the United States, "The Divine Spirit has descended once more on a man Krishnamurti, who in his lifetime is literally perfect as those who know him can testify. The World Teacher is here." Mrs. Besant's life-long dream had come true. Her spiritual student had finally graduated.

After Krishnamurti started a new road towards enlightenment, his first step was to denounce all traditions, all cults, all religious institutions, all teachers, all centres of authority including his own Theosophical Society. In August 1929 he announced his resignation from the Society in the presence of Mrs. Besant and started his solitary journey. Describing his vision for the future he said,

"The vision is total. To me that is liberation."

After that announcement and for the rest of his life, his teachings were based on his philosophy which he stated as,

"I maintain that Truth is a pathless land, and you cannot approach it by any path whatsoever, by any religion, by any sect....Truth being limitless, unconditioned, unapproachable by any path whatsoever, cannot be organized; nor should any organization be formed to lead or to coerce people along any particular path."

After his resignation, his teacher Mrs. Besant expressed a desire to resign from the Society and become his disciple but Krishnamurti refused to accept anyone as his disciple, even the very loyal and dedicated Mrs. Besant.

Krishnamurti, for the next half of the century, travelled around the world giving lectures, meeting people from every walk of life, sharing his knowledge and wisdom. Later on his teachings were compiled and distributed by Krishnamurti Writings Inc. (KWI) whose headquarters was in Ojai, California. KWI was never a religious organization and had no hierarchy; it was an organization just to coordinate Krishnamurti's writings so that they were accessible to the people who had a keen interest in his speeches, dialogues and writings.

It is difficult to summarise Krishnamurti's fifty years of teachings in a few words but it is safe to say that he stood for human freedom, decency and liberation. He had a secular philosophy and wanted every human being to follow their own heart and discover their own road.

Krishnamurti was against all organized religions because he felt that they were based on belief and that that belief hindered human growth and evolution and restricted human beings from experiencing life more freely. He also believed that religions divide rather than unite people and although leaders of those institutions preach brotherhood, in reality they set the stage for holy wars.

"Belief invariably separates. If you have a belief, or when you seek security in your particular belief, you become separated from those who seek security in some other form of belief. All organized beliefs are based on separation,

though they may preach brotherhood."

Krishnamurti was also against nationalism. He did not believe in the sanctity of geographical boundaries. He believed that nationalistic sentiments also divide people and sow feelings of anger, resentment and even hatred. Talking about feelings of nationalism he said,

"Outwardly it brings about divisions between people, classifications, wars and destruction, which is obvious to anyone who is observant. Inwardly, psychologically, this identification with the greater, with the country, with an idea, is obviously a form of self-expansion."

Krishnamurti believed that all traditions were obstacles for human evolution because they kept human beings bound to the past. He wanted human minds to be future-oriented so that they could be creative and discover new solutions to old problems. He believed that those human beings who are successful in overcoming the conditioning of their families, religions and communities are free to lead a liberated life and discover a new harmony with their environment. Such people have a fresh and novel relationship not only with people in their lives but also with animals, birds, winds, oceans, jungles and other parts of nature. In such a state of mind, even watching a palm leaf becomes a spiritual experience, an act of love.

K. Sohail

"Do you see the beauty of this? You know, just as to see the beauty of a palm leaf in the clear sky, to see it, not as an observer with all his peculiar knowledge and importance, but to look at it without the observer, to see the extraordinary movement of that palm leaf—so in the same way, to look is to learn. And in that learning is the total movement of life in which there is no fragmentation, and therefore it is a life of great harmony, and harmony means love."

All his life Krishnamurti dreamt of the day when human minds would be free from the conditioning of thousands of years of memory and able to transcend their limitations and experience that silence in which they became in touch with Ultimate Truth, which produces a unique sense of contentment.

"What man needs is that contentment that is in the earth when it has given birth to a tree. In a bush when it has produced a flower."

He believed that world chaos was the projection of individual chaos and we would not be able to achieve world peace until every human being discovered peace at a personal level.

Krishnamurti believed that even humanistic philosophy was only a partial solution to human problems because it was helpful only to control the injustices of the world, it did not do much to raise human consciousness that is the ultimate goal of human evolution.

During his interview with John White for his book, *What Is Enlightenment?*, the following exchange took place:

White: "I'll just say there are many humanitarian people and organisations feeding the hungry, treating the sick, clothing the poor and so forth."
Krishnamurti: "Humanitarianism is not changing the consciousness of men."
White: "Does that mean humanitarian works are no good?"
Krishnamurti: "No, they partly help to relieve suffering. But they don't alter human consciousness. We're talking about a radical mutation in consciousness."

Krishnamurti believed that "every cell in the human brain holds memory of the million years of man" and he asked the most fundamental question that can be asked about human nature and evolution: "Can there be total transformation in that?" Krishnamurti believed in asking those questions for which we have found no answers because that was the only way to grow, to be creative, to be spiritual.

Krishnamurti, all his life was a source of inspiration for many politicians, scientists, artists and mystics.

After the independence of India from British rule, Jawaharlal Nehru became the first prime minister. Because of all the political turbulence and personal challenges he was facing he approached Krishnamurti to seek his guidance.

K. Sohail

During their dialogue Nehru asked, "Tell me, sir, I wish to be clear of this confusion within me. Tell me what is right action and what is right thought."

Krishnamurti, after thinking for the longest time said, "Right action is only possible when the mind is silent and there is a seeing of 'what is'. Action that arises from this seeing is free of motive, of the past, free of thought and cause."

On another occasion he told Nehru, "Without self-knowledge there is no basis for right thought and action."

When Indira Gandhi became the Prime Minister she followed the tradition of her father in consulting Krishnamurti for support, guidance and wisdom.

At one time when the problem of Punjab was getting out of control she wrote, "Respected Krishnaji, I don't know what to write because I am so full of anguish. I have the feeling that I have strayed onto an unknown planet... I treasure our brief meetings. Indira"

Krishnamurti responded, "My dear Indiraji, I am very sorry indeed that you are disturbed and distressed. The world is upside down, terrible things are happening, threat of nuclear war, murder, torture, and all the unspeakable things that are taking place. It is all becoming more and more insane, and I am most concerned that you are involved in all this.

"If it is in any way, 'in any way' helpful to you, I'll come to Delhi.

Please accept my love.

J.K."

From Islam to Secular Humanism

When Indira Gandhi felt insecure and declared a state of emergency in the country, Krishnamurti, who was a supporter of human freedom, suggested to her to do the right thing and not worry about the consequences. Indira Gandhi subsequently decided to end the Emergency status of the country. Pupul Jayakar, Krishnamurti's biographer who also knew Indira Gandhi very well, wrote about Indira Gandhi's reaction in these words, "In later years she told me that it was on October 28, 1976, the day she met Krishnaji for the second time, a frail movement had awakened in her, suggesting an end to the Emergency, whatever the consequences. She had mulled over this feeling, talked to a few people close to her, and finally took the decision to call an election."

When the Dalai Lama was visiting India he came especially to meet Krishnamurti and after the meeting commented, "A great soul, a great experience."

During one of his trips to Europe, Krishnamurti met the famous English playwright George Bernard Shaw, who after the meeting described him as "the most beautiful human being [he] had ever met."

During his stay in California he spent a lot of time with Aldous Huxley who later wrote an introduction to his book, *The First And Last Freedom*. After listening to one of Krishnamurti's speeches Huxley described it in a letter,

> "...as amongst the most impressive things I have listened to, it was like listening to the discourse of the Buddha—such power, such intrinsic authority...."

K. Sohail

In one of his dialogues Huxley confessed to Krishnamurti, "that (he) would give everything for one direct perception of the truth, but his mind was incapable of it. It was too filled with knowledge."

Even Henry Miller whose books were banned in America for twenty-five years because of their sexually specific content wrote about Krishnamurti after reading a book about him by Carlo Suarez, "Krishnamurti has renounced more than any man I can think of except Christ. Fundamentally he is so simple to understand that it is easy to comprehend the confusion which his clear, direct words and deeds have entailed. Men are reluctant to accept what is easy to grasp.

"I have never met Krishnamurti, though there is no man living whom I would consider it a greater privilege to meet than he.

"He liberated his soul, so to say, from the underworld and the overworld, thus opening to it 'the paradise of heroes.' Is it necessary to define this state?"

Krishnamurti died in February 1986 at the age of 90. His body was cremated according to his will and his ashes divided into three equal parts, to be buried in California, England and India. Krishnamurti did not want a monument to be built as he believed that teachings were more important than the teacher.

From Islam to Secular Humanism

References:

1. Jayakar, Papul. *Krishnamurti –A Biography*, Harper and Row Publishers, New York, 1985.
2. Krishnamurti. *The First and Last Freedom*, Krishnamurti Foundation, London, 1986.
3. White, John, Editor. *What is Enlightenment?* Jeremy Tarcher Inc., Los Angeles, 1984.

K. Sohail

Insanity and Spirituality

One of the important questions in mysticism is: "How do we differentiate between spiritual and psychotic experiences?" When we study the description of those experiences and the analyses by mental health professionals we find that there are some similarities and some differences. The similarities are that the mystic and the psychotic both claim that they are in touch with God and are getting direct special messages from him. They both experience loss of ego boundaries. They both become transformed by those experiences. The differences are that in a mystic:

- the experiences are a part of self-hypnosis
- they are completely reversible
- they are associated with a sense of euphoria and well being
- they improve the self esteem of the person and help the person to integrate their life at a higher level of maturity.

They are growth-promoting experiences for the person and the community.

On the other hand the psychotic experiences are

associated with a lot of emotional pain and suffering and gradually lead to the disintegration of the personality and lifestyle of the person.

Maitreya, a twentieth-century mystic, who claimed to be the re-birth of Buddha, in his book of revelations, *The Gospel of Peace* writes, "The birth of every scripture seems to be tied with, and is a product of, the spiritual re-birthing of the individual, of experiencing the state which is known by a variety of names, as I said in the beginning: the nirvanic state, enlightenment, satori, self-realization, un-ul-haq, illumination, re-birth, realizing the supra-mental or cosmic consciousness." He shares one of his experiences:

"Then, about two months later, around 4:00 in the early hours of the morning I was awakened by the same divine presence, and a voice spoke to me 'take thy pen and write. 'I' shall speak to you the last book. The Gospel of Peace. Start with the beginning.
There was no beginning. 'I' never created anything. There was no moment of birth, nor shall be one of death; of the universe. Do not be confused and write. 'I' never created anything outside and apart from 'MYSELF'..."

In mystic literature there have been two parallel traditions, 'hama oust'...Everything is Him and 'hama az oust'...Everything is from Him. One tradition believes that the whole universe has one cosmic holy unity while the other considers that the universe was created and is separate from the creator. Maitreya, who was also known as Dr. Honda, was a professor at the University of Toronto in 1980s and led a productive life till his death in 1990.

On the other hand, one of my young patients who suffered from schizophrenia used to be preoccupied by religious and spiritual matters and as his condition deteriorated his life started to disintegrate. He had very poor self-esteem. He believed he was ugly and nobody liked him. Unfortunately his condition did not respond to medications, psychotherapy or even hospitalization.

One day he showed me one of his poems, which read,

> Here at home
> come inside my name is hell
> let me give you pain and agony so you won't feel well
> over in the distance across the flames of darkness you can here a bell
> I welcome you into my fear I see you like it I can tell
> up from God in heaven above I was defeated and fell
> down to the stinking creation God made
> I sit here down on earth a demon of hade
> I hate man's soul and make him to fade
> into the night the dark gloom and shade
> death destruction is my name and confusion and death on earth all of it will I claim
> the war pains grace in man's head—take a look around and know my name
> the name of satan is of hell, fury furnace reign
> God is but a dove, yet I am the dragon and crush his weak wings all over each I claim suffering and life, love of greed

> I sing
> I love the danger of battle the screams of man in my ear I love to hear it ring
> against spikes and stakes—God's people will I crush and fling
> come into me satan and darken my soul
> down here in my hell for inside my home.

This young schizophrenic was so tormented by his psychotic and religious experiences that a few months after writing that poem he committed suicide.

Silvano Arieti, a famous American psychiatrist, comments on the differences of psychotic and mystical experiences:

> "Mystical experiences seem to correspond to what are called hallucinations and delusions in psychiatric terms—it is easy to confuse religious mystics with psychotic patients especially those psychotics who have hallucinations and delusions with a religious content."

Arieti feels that there are marked differences between them. He writes,

> "The individual who experiences them (mystical experiences) has a marked rise in self-esteem and a sense of his being or becoming a worthwhile and very active person. He has been given a mission, a special insight, and from now on he must be on the move doing something important— more important than his life.

K. Sohail

"In mystical experiences we have a tradition of auto-hypnosis. A subject puts himself into a state of a trance and projects power to the divinity. ...The hypnosis is time limited and totally reversible.

"The hallucinatory and delusional experiences of the schizophrenic are generally accompanied by a more or less apparent disintegration of the whole person. Religious and mystical experiences seem to result in a strengthening and enriching of the personality."

John White, editor of a book What is Enlightenment? like some other mystics, believes that a nervous breakdown with loss of ego boundaries, paranoia and other symptoms of mental illness might be a transitory step towards a breakthrough. Those people who cannot go to the next stage become mentally ill while those who are lucky to be guided by a teacher or guru to the next stage finally experience a breakthrough and achieve nirvana and enlightenment. He shares his philosophy in these words,

"The marvellous thing about us as nature-becoming-aware-of-itself-as-God is that each of us has the latent ability to take conscious control of our own evolution, to build our own bridge, and thereby become a member of the new age, the new humanity.

In the course of this change, there are stages that can be presented in a simple formulation: from arthonoia through paranoia to metanoia. We grow from arthonoia—that is, the common, every day state of ego centred

mind—to metanoia only by going through paranoia, a state in which the mind is deranged within (that is, taken apart) and rearranged through spiritual discipline so that clear perception of reality might be experienced. Conventional western psychologists regard paranoia as a pathological breakdown. It often is, of course, but seen from this perspective, it is not necessarily so. Rather, it can be a breakthrough—not the final breakthrough, to be sure, but a necessary stage of development on the way to realizing the kingdom.

Paranoia is a condition well understood by mystical and sacred traditions. The spiritual disciplines that people practise under the guidance of guru or master are designed to ease and quicken the passage through paranoia so that the practitioner doesn't get lost in the labyrinth of inner space and become a casualty.

Because metanoia has by large not been experienced by the founders of western psychology and psychotherapy, paranoia has not been fully understood in our culture. It is seen as an aberrant dead end rather than a necessary precondition to higher consciousness. It is not understood that the confusion, discomfort, and suffering experienced in paranoia are due entirely to the destruction of an illusion, ego. The less we cling to that illusion, the less we suffer."

It is interesting to note that neither do all psychotics have religious experiences nor do all mystics experience a psychotic breakdown.

The question can be asked, if a mystic has psychotic

experiences or a psychotic claims to have mystical experiences would they need to see a spiritual guru or a mental health therapist? Is the problem mental or spiritual? And who is the expert to answer that question? And how would we know that the answer is not a reflection of the bias of the expert?

It is unfortunate that most mystics do not have an in-depth knowledge and experience of working with mentally ill people and most mental health professionals do not have a keen interest in religious and spiritual matters. Most clergy and mental health professionals do not see eye to eye about many issues of human sufferings. I find it quite interesting that the word psyche that used to mean soul now means mind in the western world. As I stated at the beginning of this book, I feel that religious practices and philosophies and mental health practices and philosophies are co-existing as two banks of the river. I think the time has come to build bridges to join those two banks and open channels of communication so that the experts on both sides can share their knowledge, experiences and wisdom for the benefit of all people.

Being a student of human psychology and having a keen interest in human spirituality, I feel that the roles of gurus and therapists are not mutually exclusive. I think they compliment each other. They have similarities and differences. They just operate on two extremes of the human condition. On one side are the issues of human suffering. When people are overwhelmed by the pressures and stresses of life and experience anxiety, depression, paranoia or other symptoms of emotional disorder and mental illness, they need the care and compassion of mental health professionals who can help them with medications and different kinds of psychotherapy to control their symptoms. On the other extreme are those people who are preoccupied with the issue of quality of life. They are dealing with the existential dilemma of personal growth. They want to improve their lifestyles and want to live at the highest level of their potential. In such cases spiritual teachers can help them to achieve enlightenment. It is interesting to see that just as a therapist may not accept a client for in-depth psychotherapy if the client does not have ego-strength or genuine motivation, in the same way a mystic may not accept someone as his disciple if the pupil is not strong enough to endure the hardships of a spiritual journey or is not sincere and has some ulterior motives.

I feel there is an area of the personal growth of human beings where the role of a growth-oriented therapist and a spiritual teacher overlap. They both want people to travel on the road of self-actualization. Because they belong to different traditions historically, they use a different language and vocabulary. Psychotherapy is the product of western scientific thinking while mysticism has been the outcome of the eastern spiritual tradition.

Erich Fromm in his article about Zen Buddhism and psychoanalysis writes,

"But in spite of the fact that both psychoanalysis and Zen deal with the nature of man and with a practice leading to his transformation, the differences seem to outweigh these similarities. Psychoanalysis is a scientific method, nonreligious to its core.

Zen is a theory and technique to achieve 'enlightenment' an experience which in the West would be called religious or mystical. Psychoanalysis is a therapy for mental illness; Zen a way of spiritual salvation."

References

1. Maitreya. *The Gospel of Peace*, Universal Way Publications, Canada, 1988.
2. Sohail, K. *Schizophrenia*, Gora Publishers, Pakistan, 1992.
3. Arieti, Silvano. *Interpretation of Schizophrenia*, Basic Books, New York, 1974.
4. Fromm, Erich. Suzuki, D.T. and DeMartino, Richard. *Zen Buddhism and Psychoanalysis*, Harper Colophon Books, New York, 1960.
5. White, John. *What Is Enlightenment?*, Jermey Tarcher Inc., Los Angeles, 1984.

Mystic Poetry

Mystic poetry has a unique position in the family of world literature because it focuses on:
- internal rather than external realities,
- inner rather than outer truths,
- metaphysical rather than physical journeys, and
- spiritual rather than materialistic worlds.

Mystic poets accept the ultimate challenge of describing the indescribable, giving form to the formless. They ask themselves:

How do we talk about a world
    where sounds turn mute?
How do we write about a world
    where words lose all their meanings?
How do we discuss a world
    that transcends every logic?
How do we describe a world
    that has no boundaries?
How do we conceptualize a world
    that defies any form?

How do we understand a world
 that is beyond words and sounds
and colours and space and time
 and logic and.................?

and answer it in the words of Tagore,

"I dive down into the depths of the ocean of forms, hoping to gain the perfect pearl of the formless." (Ref. 1)

Mystic poets are those enlightened beings who have personal encounters with the spiritual world and have touched the borders of known with the unknown, human with the divine, personal with the cosmic. They share with us that their experiences are intimate encounters with a world which is nameless, formless, timeless and pathless.

"No miseries befall one who does not cling to name and form." ~ Buddha (Ref. 2)

"Sufiism is truth without form." ~ Ibn-e-Jalali (Ref. 3)

"Pass from time and place to timelessness and placelessness, to other worlds. There is our origin."
~ Samarqandi Amini (Ref. 3)

"Truth is a pathless land." ~ Krishnamurti (Ref. 4)

K. Sohail

When mystic poets express themselves in poetry they are more concerned about sharing their spiritual experiences, mystical encounters and existential truths and less preoccupied with the technique, form and language of their presentation. They are quite aware that they are not trying to impress their readers with scholarship, they are trying to help them open their inner eyes which will get in touch with their own personal truths.

When we study mystic poetry created throughout the world over the centuries, we come across certain master symbols that have a universal value because they are created from the body of human experience.

The first master symbol we come across is water. Water is one of the most significant ingredients of human existence. It not only gives birth to life, it also sustains it. Most of the human body is made of water. When water takes the form of an ocean, it becomes deep and mysterious and only the daring ones have the courage to descend into its depths. Mystics are the ones who risk going to the bottom of the ocean of life to come back with the pearls of wisdom and tranquillity.

Mystic poets see a human being, human self and human consciousness as a drop of water and the eternal truth and cosmic consciousness as an ocean. They claim that an ordinary man can see drops of water in an ocean but one needs special awareness and consciousness to see an ocean in a drop of water.

From Islam to Secular Humanism

Kabir Das said,
> "A *drop*
> *is merged*
> *into the ocean*
> *that everyone*
> *understands;*
> *but how*
> *the ocean*
> *is contained*
> *in the drop*
> *that, O my friend*
> *only a rare man*
> *can comprehend."* (Ref. 5)

The second master symbol we come across in mystic poetry is fire. Mystic poets feel that travelling on the spiritual path is like jumping into the fire of love. If one is honest and sincere, fire transforms into a rose garden and the traveller embraces the ultimate truth; but if the traveller is an amateur and is just curious about the spiritual path then he can easily get burnt.

Rumi said,
> *"Love is that flame that*
> *when it is kindled*
> *burns everything away*
> *God only remains."* (Ref. 6)

K. Sohail

Kabir Das shared,
> *"This seeking*
> *O friend*
> *is a stupendous task,*
> *a raging fire*
> *it is.*
> *Jump in*
> *if you wish*
> *to be baked*
> *but if you are*
> *merely curious*
> *this fire*
> *would destroy you."* (Ref. 5)

Playing with fire can be seen as adventure but also a dangerous phenomenon. Only those who have confidence in themselves and in their love can dare to go close to it. But once mystics embrace the flame then they are sure that they will be cleansed from all those impurities that are hindrances in their spiritual journey. Fire purifies things not only in our day-to-day lives but also our souls, in our spiritual lives.

William Blake wrote,
> *"Unless the eye catch fire*
> *the God will not be seen*
> *unless the ear catch fire*
> *the God will not be heard*
> *unless the tongue catch fire*

the God will not be named
unless the heart catch fire
the God will not be loved
unless the mind catch fire
the God will not be known." (Ref. 5)

The third master symbol we come across in mystic poetry is light. Mystic poets highlight that after travelling in the dark alleys of one's soul and on convoluted paths of the spiritual labyrinth, human beings reach a stage where they discover their inner light.

Kabir Das,
"I shall make
my body into
a clay-lamp,
my soul, its wick
and my blood oil
ah, the light
of this lamp
would reveal
the face
of my beloved
to me." (Ref. 5)

In this journey the traveller has to consume himself to discover light and be enlightened.

K. Sohail

Baba Farid-ad-din Attar wrote,
> *"The true lover finds the light only if,*
> *like the candle*
> *he is his own fuel*
> *consuming himself."* (Ref. 7)

Anonymous,
> *"First you go toward the light*
> *Next you are in the light*
> *Then you are the light."* (Ref. 4)

Alongside light being a guide in the darkest journeys of our inner self, it is also a synthesis of the colours of the rainbow. When different aspects of human life merge in people then they become enlightened beings and then their thoughts, words and actions become a source of light for others. They become torches that guide the lost souls.

After discovering the inner truth and light mystics tend to speak less and avoid arguments. They prefer to remain quiet. They realize that their genuine silence can communicate more than idle talk or meaningless debates. They become aware of the limitations of words.

Madhu Lal Hussain said,
> *"Be never engaged at all*
> *in arguments so long*
> *but ponder over your end*
> *so says Hussain Faqir."* (Ref. 7)

Kabir Das wrote,
> "*Anyone who had a taste*
> *of his love*
> *is so enchanted by it*
> *that he is stricken*
> *with silence.*
> *O dear friend*
> *when you have a gem*
> *in your hand*
> *you don't go*
> *on the street*
> *announcing it.*" (Ref. 5)

While studying mystic poetry we are also struck by the simplicity of the expression. Mystic poets use simple language because they want to communicate with common people. They don't want to impress literary scholars and critics. They are humble people and their humility is reflected in their poetry. They know the art of expressing the most profound experiences in the simplest ways. Rather, they are dissatisfied with those scholars and clergy who use difficult language that common people cannot understand. They feel it reflects their elitist attitude and arrogance. Mystics are critical of those pandits, maulvis, priests and rabbis who give sermons in a foreign language and offer prayers in Sanskrit, Latin, Hebrew or Arabic that the masses do not comprehend. Mystics resent those rituals and dogmas that distance people from their own truths and establish the authority of religious institutions. Mystics encourage people to communicate and pray in their mother tongues or meditate in silence.

Many mystics feel that knowledge rather than helping to find enlightenment can often become a hindrance in one's spiritual growth. Aldous Huxley confessed to Krishnamurti that, "He would give everything for one direct perception of the truth, but his mind was incapable of it. It was too filled with knowledge." (Ref. 8)

When we study Kabir's poetry we find that being a weaver by profession, he like many other mystic poets, identified with working class people so much that his poetry is full of symbols and metaphors derived from the crafts—weaving, pottery, farming and other working class professions. He also weaves his verses with phenomena of nature so that common people can relate to his poetry.

When we study the life stories of mystic poets we become aware that many of them led simple lives. Because of their aptitude and personalities they did not fit into the formal education systems and traditional institutions of their times. They were the students of the university of life and learnt from their own experiences. They followed the trails of their own hearts and souls rather than the highways of tradition and convention. One such example is Walt Whitman, a mystic poet of nineteenth-century America who has influenced twentieth-century American literature more than any other poet. Although his poems from his collection *Leaves of Grass* are taught in colleges and universities all over the world, he himself did not do well in school. His teacher, Mr. Benjamin Halleck, was so

---

From Islam to Secular Humanism

disappointed in him that he told his father, "This boy is so idle, I am sure he will never amount to anything."

Whitman's father, agreeing with the teacher, took him out of school at age thirteen and asked him to work in a printer's shop. Even at work he was so preoccupied with his soul-searching that his employer thought that he was devoting himself to "the fine art of doing nothing." (Ref. 9)

Teacher, employer, and father as well as many other people, failed to realise that Walt Whitman was trying to contemplate and meditate upon the mysteries of life from a very early age.

Mystic poets and their poetry have been a mystery and a source of controversy for traditional literary critics. When we study the reviews of mystic poetry, on one hand we find those who evaluate such poetry as containing lack of form, style and literary beauty, while others consider mystic poetry a different genre and insist that it should not be considered a part of ordinary poetry because of the nature of poetry and personalities of the mystics. They consider saints, sufis and mystics more visionaries than poets.

Sehdev Kumar, a research scholar of the poetry of Kabir Das wrote, "...Kabir was first and foremost a visionary, his poetry is a mere 'by-product of his vision'...Kabir is a nirgunibhakta—a lover of the formless and infinite," and as such it should not be judged as poetry. The verses of the saints are of an entirely different genre than those of the poets. From the pen of William Kingland, we read:

"The mystic may not always be a master of language, but it is truth which he endeavours to express that we should do well to seize; and learn also to make proper allowance for the inadequacy of language to express the deepest truths. No one knows better than the greatest master of technique how inadequate are the materials with which he has to work, no one realizes more clearly than the greatest master of language, how little language can express of the living truth with which his innermost nature is on fire."
(Ref. 5)

Rumi said,
> "You see through each cloak I wear
> know if I speak without mouth or language
> the world is drunk on its desire for words
> I am the slave of the Master of silence." (Ref. 6)

References

1. Tagore, Rabindranath. *Gitanjali*, MacMillan Publishers Ltd., London, England, 1913.
2. Buddha. *Dhammapada*, Translation by Thomas Cleary, Bantam Books, New York, 1995.
3. Shah, Idries. *The Way of the Sufi*, Penguin Books, England, 1968.
4. White, John, Editor. *What Is Enlightenment?*, Jeremy Tarcher Inc., Los Angeles, 1984.
5. Kumar, Sehdev. *The Vision of Kabir*, Alpha and Omega Books, Ontario, Canada, 1984.
6. Harvey, Andrew. *Love's Fire - Re-creations of Rumi*, Meeramma Publications, New York, 1988.
7. Rehman, Tariq, Editor. *Mystic Poets of Pakistan*, Pakistan Academy of Letters, Islamabad, 1993.
8. Jayakar, Pupul. *Krishnamurti - A Biography*, Harper and Row Publishers, New York, 1986.
9. Thomas, Henry and Thomas, Dana Lees. *Living Biographies of Great Poets*, Garden City Books, New York, 1984.

K. Sohail

Secular Humanism

When I was a young boy I had heard the story of an old Indian man who was observed planting trees which would bear mangos, his favourite fruit. Someone asked him "You know that mango trees take seven years to bear fruit and you will not be alive to taste them, so why are you planting them?" He responded with an affectionate smile on his wrinkled face, "They are for my grandchildren."

Whether they be mango trees or trees of knowledge and wisdom, sharing the fruits of one's lifelong struggles with coming generations is a special gift and that sharing happens in the context of intergenerational loving relationships.

When I lived in the East, I did not fully appreciate the special relationship children have with their grandparents, aunts and uncles, quite different than the relationship they have with their parents. An extended family system provides a natural environment for multiple role models. Teenagers can share incidents, ask questions and have an honest and open dialogue with their aunts and uncles that they are reluctant to have with their own parents. Those aunts and uncles play a significant role in their emotional, intellectual and philosophical development.

Living in the West, I sometimes miss those relationships because most people live in the Nuclear or Single Parent rather than Extended family system. Whenever I go to Pakistan, I enjoy the special relationship I have with my aunts and uncles. So when my nephew initiated a dialogue about his religious doubts and philosophical questions, I found an opportunity to share my values with him, the same way my uncle had shared them with me when I was young. I sometimes wish teenagers in the Western world could enjoy the same kind of special relationships with their aunts and uncles as I had living in the East. Such relationships keep the channels of communication open. They provide an opportunity for knowledge and wisdom to be passed freely and affectionately from one generation to the next. My nephew inspired me to write the last chapter of my book. That is why I dedicated my book to him. My uncle, the author of nearly twenty books, had dedicated his last collection of poems to me. He perceived me the way I perceive my nephew, the representative of the next generation.

My dear nephew Zeeshan!

Last month when I was visiting Pakistan, I was quite fascinated by your keen interest in philosophy. I felt honoured when one morning before leaving for school, you asked me if I could go out with you for dinner and discuss some of your concerns about traditional religion. When we met at the Copper Kettle that evening, I was impressed how openly and honestly you shared your confusion, your conflicts and your debates with your religious friends. That evening I was so reminded of my meeting with my uncle, Arif Abdul Mateen, nearly thirty years ago, when I was a student in Medical College. Last year when I was interviewed by Suad Sharabani for a program on CBC Radio, I had talked about that meeting and its effect on me.

"In those days I used to live with my parents in Peshawar and my uncle lived in Lahore. By that time he knew that I had been studying his books of poetry and was writing poems and short stories myself. He came to visit us for a few days and one day he took me out to have a cup of tea and talk to me. I was surprised because in those days there was no tradition of taking people out, especially children and teenagers. We went to the Greens, a posh hotel in the cantonment and he ordered tea and snacks. We had a heart to heart talk. It was a special meeting for me. My uncle was very affectionate and thoughtful. He treated me like a young adult rather than a child. That day I opened my heart to him and shared all my doubts and fears, dilemmas and dreams. I shared with him all the conflicts I was experiencing between scientific knowledge I was gaining at the university and the religious traditions I had grown up with. I also shared with him that whenever I discuss my doubts with people around me I am asked to have blind faith.

"My uncle listened to my story patiently and then said, 'Sohail! You have to accept that you are a member of a family who has always chosen a non-traditional path. Your grandfather left the highway of tradition when he was sixty; I left it when I was forty and I feel pleased and proud that you are leaving it when you are twenty. Try to discover the trail of your heart. There is no need of being rebellious and confrontative and trying to convince others. That will alienate you from your family. You are still a student and you need to live with them until you finish your education. After that you can do whatever your heart desires. At this stage don't worry about right and wrong. It is not the destination that is important, it is the journey that matters. It is the process that is significant.'

"After that meeting I felt as though a big weight had

been lifted from my shoulders. I felt light. I could fly like a bird. He told me that in every community there have been poets and mystics and philosophers who have chosen the trail rather than the highway and they have suffered for it. It has always taken people a long time to appreciate their worth."

Last week when you wrote me a long letter sharing your philosophy and belief system and asked me to share my views about Secular Humanism, God, Scriptures, Prophets, Religion and Morality with you, I started to think about those issues once again and was inspired to write this letter. I am quite aware that it is not easy to express one's views in a few words on those profound issues. Philosophers have written lengthy books on those topics. I will make a humble attempt to share some of my ideas and glimpses of my philosophical and ideological evolution. I am quite aware that I am still searching and growing. I feel fortunate that I have discovered a sense of peace within myself and being a writer have found ways to share the highlights of my journey with others.

Humanism

I have shared my ideas and dreams in the introduction of my book *Pages of My Heart* in these words,

> *"I think that we have reached such a turning point in history where we are forced to make certain choices individually and collectively.*

I hope that we do not proceed on the path of self-destruction which ends in collective suicide, rather we decide to discover new ways of living harmoniously with ourselves,
other human beings,
and Mother Nature.

Perhaps one day we will reach that state of communal growth and human evolution where we can accept that whether they are children or the elderly, women or minorities, the physically disabled or mentally sick, all human beings have a right to live respectfully and grow peacefully. For our future development as a species we have to transcend the resentments based on class, race, gender, language or religious differences and anger because of the conflicts between East and West, North and South, First and Third world and many other man-made divisions. Sooner or later we have to accept that we are all human, members of the same family, and our enemies are part of us, just distant cousins.

I am quite aware that these are my personal and global dreams, but I believe that we are the products of our dreams. When our dreams are shattered we start to disintegrate individually and collectively."

God

There was a time I used to believe in a Personal God. I believed in a Heavenly Father, millions of years old, with a grey beard wearing a crown sitting on a throne in seventh heaven, waiting on a crisis line, personally answering his distressed children's prayers day and night. I believed God had created the whole universe and He was a form of physical reality. Over the years my belief system and philosophy have changed. I no longer believe God is a physical reality.

But as a student of human psychology and cultural studies, I have also become aware that we as human beings also live in another reality:

a reality that is personal and private,

a reality that is abstract and symbolic,

a reality that is created by our own imagination.

Such realities are fictional and metaphorical and are the birthing place of fiction, folklore and mythology.

Such realities differ in different parts of the world.

Such realities give us insight into the psyche of those cultures.

Human history tells us that concepts of God have existed as those kinds of realities.

In some cultures we have a male God, in others we have female Goddesses.

In some cultures God is fatherly and punitive, in others, God is motherly and nurturing.

In some cultures God is abstract, in others God appears as man-made statues and idols.

In some cultures God is perceived as a Creator and is believed to exist outside the universe. In others people say All That Exists Is God.

From Islam to Secular Humanism

In some cultures people believe God lives within all of us, and we do not need to believe in Him to know and experience Him.

In others people believe we are all Gods in the making.

Living in different cultures and travelling in others, I came to believe that rather than saying Man was created in God's image, it might be wiser to say that God was created in Man's image and that the qualities assigned to God or Allah or Bhagwan or Great Mystery are reflections of the human psyche of that era and culture. There are no two human beings or cultures in the whole wide world that have a similar concept or experience of the reality. For those who project their fears and insecurities, God becomes a Rorschach Test and for those who project their fantasies, dreams and ideals, God becomes a Santa Claus.

There is a time human beings as children believe in Santa Claus, but then they grow up and learn to buy their own toys while they fulfill their own dreams and follow their own ideals.

It is also interesting that people who do not believe in a Personal God in ordinary circumstances, start praying in a crisis. That is why Erica Jong once wrote, "There are no atheists in turbulent airplanes."

There was a time I believed in an omnipotent God who performed miracles, but now I believe that the universe around us runs according to the laws of nature and the more we are aware of those laws, the more we can understand and change our personal and social lives. Now I believe that with the advancement of biological and social sciences, our understanding of our inner and outer universes is expanding and we as human beings are becoming more aware, evolved and enlightened.

I am also realizing that human experiences are more authentic than belief systems. Buddha believed, "One's own experience is the ultimate teacher."

When Krishnamurti was asked, "Belief in God has been a powerful incentive to better living. Why do you deny God? Why do you not try to revive man's faith in the idea of God?" he responded,

"Let us look at the problem widely and intelligently. I am not denying God—it would be foolish to do so. Only the man who does not know reality indulges in meaningless words. The man who says he knows, does not know; the man who is experiencing reality from moment to moment has no means of communicating that reality.

Belief is a denial of truth, belief hinders truth, to believe in God is not to find God. Neither the believer nor the non-believer will find God; because the reality is the unknown, and your belief or non-belief in the unknown is merely a self-projection and therefore not real. I know you believe and I know it has very little meaning in your life. There are many people who believe; millions believe in God and take consolation. First of all, why do you believe? You believe because it gives you satisfaction, consolation, hope, and you say it gives you significance in life. Actually your belief has very little significance, because you believe and exploit, you believe and kill, you believe in a universal

> *God and murder each other. The rich man also believes in God; he exploits ruthlessly, accumulates money, and then builds a temple or becomes a philanthropist.*
>
> *The men who dropped the atomic bomb on Hiroshima said God was with them, those who flew from England to destroy Germany said that God was their co-pilot. The dictators, the prime ministers, the generals, the presidents, all talk to God, they have immense faith in God. Are they doing service, making a better life for man? The people who say they believe in God have destroyed half of the world and the world is in complete misery."* (Ref. 1, p205)

Krishnamurti very eloquently highlighted that people's actions are more important than their belief systems. That is why there is the common belief that, "Actions speak louder than words."

I sometimes wonder whether the expression, the word, the term, the concept GOD, over the centuries, has lost all its meaning and creates more confusion than clarity in our dialogues and the search for our personal truths, truths that are better experienced than described and debated.

Prophets

I remember the days when I believed that Prophets were messengers of God and were blessed with divine revelations. I believed they performed miracles. Gradually I realized that they were special people who wanted to reform societies and improve the quality of life for their communities. They tried their best to reduce suffering in the world and hoped that people would get in touch with the spiritual aspects of themselves and travel on the road of enlightenment. Prophets with their own lifestyles became a source of inspiration and a role model for millions of people.

Of all the books that I have read about Prophets, the one that impressed me the most was written by a Canadian psychiatrist, Dr. Richard Bucke. It is called *Cosmic Consciousness*. I have recommended it to many friends who have a keen interest in understanding the psychology of prophets and mystics. In that book Dr. Bucke presents a hypothesis that consciousness, over the centuries, has passed through three stages of evolution.

The first stage he calls Simple Consciousness which is present in animals. Animals know.

The second stage is Self Consciousness. Dr. Bucke believes that Self Consciousness differentiates humans from animals. Human beings *know that they know*. Such a quality has helped human beings to create language. Bucke feels that in the early phase of evolution, only a few must have acquired that consciousness but over thousands of years, it has become universal.

The third stage is Cosmic Consciousness. That stage has been acquired by only a few in human history. Some of those people that history calls prophets, mystics, philosophers and artists have acquired that level of consciousness. Bucke provides a detailed analysis of biographies of such people all the way from Buddha to Walt Whitman and highlights special features of their

---

From Islam to Secular Humanism

personalities. Bucke feels that over the next few thousand years, more and more people will acquire cosmic consciousness and "in contact with the flux of cosmic consciousness all religions known and named today will be melted down." (Ref. 2, p. 5)

Bucke feels people in society can be divided into two groups: people with lower mind and people with higher mind. He differentiates between them in these words:

> "*The lower mind then lacks faith, lacks courage, lacks personal force, lacks sympathy, lacks affection.... That is (to sum up) it lacks peace, contentment, happiness....*
>
> *On the other hand, the higher mind (as compared with the lower) possesses faith, courage, personal force, sympathy, affection; that is, it possesses (relatively) happiness, is less prone to fear of things known and unknown and anger and hatred ... that is to unhappiness.*" (Ref. 2, p. 41)

Bucke is optimistic that as time passes, more and more human beings will develop Cosmic Consciousness, and one day it will become universal. He wrote,

> "*In our ancestry, self consciousness dates back to the first true man. Thousands of years must have elapsed between its first appearance and its universality, just as thousands of years are now passing between the first cases of cosmic consciousness and its universality.*" (Ref. 2, p. 47)

K. Sohail

Religions

Prophets experienced personal truths and shared them with others. Unfortunately most of their followers who were not as enlightened as those prophets, tried to institutionalize those truths and gave birth to religions. Those religions saved the traditions with all their morals and rituals but lost touch with their essence, their spirit. The self-proclaimed heirs of those traditions, whether they were priests, maulanas, rabbis or pandits, gained social power to declare people sinners and send them to Hell. Religions and churches became political institutions and priests with their own interpretations of scriptures became influential figures in their communities. They gained the power to judge and condemn people.

It is unfortunate to see how religions have erected walls of resentment, anger, prejudice and hatred between different communities. Krishnamurti once said, "Through religious intolerance there are divisions of people as believers and non-believers, leading to religious wars."
(Ref. 1, p. 206)

It is unfortunate that prophets who wanted to bring enlightenment and peace were followed by their disciples who advocated holy wars.

Over the years I came to realize that the true heirs of those prophets were the saints and mystics who accepted rather than judged people and tried to unite rather than divide people.

From Islam to Secular Humanism

Scriptures

There was a time I used to read scriptures like cookbooks, trying to find recipes for my day to day living.

There was a time I would read scriptures like books of law trying to discover God's penal code.

There was a time I believed that if I did not follow the scriptures, I would be judged harshly on the day of judgement and burn in Hell.

But as I grew older and started studying science, literature and philosophy, I discovered that scholars had made not only diverse but also rather conflicting and contradictory interpretations of scriptures.

Gradually I realized that the interpretations of scriptures are very subjective and most of the conflicts between different sects and religions were the result of literal interpretations of scriptures.

Now I believe that holy books are a part of a literature of wisdom that different cultures have created over the centuries. They are like folklore dealing with the spiritual dimension of life. They are a part and parcel of different cultural traditions and mythologies. Now I strongly feel that scriptures should be read to meditate in silence upon the secrets of life and should not be used as sources of debate in assembly halls to make laws to punish oneself and others or used in religious institutions to control and judge people and declare them sinners and infidels. I firmly believe that scriptures are meant for our private worlds, to be enhanced by loving and respecting one another.

K. Sohail

Morality

Over the years I have come to the realization that different people are good for different reasons and some 'goods' are better than others. I believe that there is a hierarchy of good behaviours. Some I value more highly than others.

At the lowest level is the good that is done out of *fear*. Fear is the motivating force. The child, the teenager, the adult is afraid of the consequences.

A child behaves well because he does not want to be beaten up by his angry father.

A teenager studies hard because he does not want to fail the exam.

An adult does not steal or kill because he does not want to go to Hell.

Governments and churches know that. States have police officers and churches have priests and rabbis and maulanas to send people to judgement systems to be condemned to lifelong imprisonment or an eternal hell for their bad behaviour.

In the middle are the good people who are motivated by the hope of a reward. Reward and positive consequences are the motivating force.

A child may behave well for an ice cream or mother's affection.

A teenager might conform and study hard to stand first in the class and earn a scholarship and the pride of the family.

From Islam to Secular Humanism

An adult might do good deeds to earn a handsome pay cheque, status, fame or a place in Heaven.

Each community has representatives who give good news, whether they are school principals, heads of state, or church ministers. The same priest who delivers bad news about Hell also bears good news about Heaven.

In my mind, the highest good is the one that is done for its own sake. Virtue becomes its own reward. The enjoyment, the reward, the ecstasy, stays in the act not outside. The person enjoys and feels fulfilled, while he is performing the good act.

An artist enjoys the act of creating.

A mother enjoys the process of mothering.

A teacher enjoys the act of teaching.

A nurse enjoys the act of healing others.

The reward later on is just a bonus. It is enjoyed and welcome but is not the motivating force.

I usually give the example of voluntary work people do. We can imagine three people doing voluntary work side by side.

The first one is a teenager who has been ordered by the judge to do a hundred hours of community work rather than going to jail or paying a fine.

The second one is a young adult doing the same voluntary work because he wants to put it on his resume so that he can get a job later on. He has an ulterior motive that nobody knows.

K. Sohail

The third one is a middle-aged man doing the same voluntary work because he loves people. He is not ordered by the court, and he already has a good job; but in his free time, he loves to help the poor, the sick, the needy and the disabled. He feels he is blessed for being healthy and gainfully employed, and wants to share his time, energy and money with the less privileged. He enjoys the act of giving rather than taking, the act of sharing rather than hoarding.

I believe that the responsibility of parents, teachers and representatives of social, religious, and political institutions is to help and inspire people grow from the lowest to the highest form of GOOD.

Dear Zeeshan!

I am quite aware that by addressing you, I am also addressing all those people, young or old, who are in search of their personal truths.

I believe there are two types of children: children of the flesh who inherit the biological features of their parents and children of the soul who carry the knowledge and wisdom from one generation to another. My uncle shared his artistic and spiritual values with me and I am sharing my humanistic values with you, hoping that you would share them with the next generation.

I hope my philosophical journey inspires you and others to open their hearts to new struggles, experiences and dreams. I hope we all stay young at heart and keep on growing till the day we die. I strongly believe that we grow old only when we stop growing.

Affectionately,
Sohail

References

1. Krishnamurti, J. *The First and Last Freedom*, Harper and Row Publishers New York, 1975.
2. Bucke, Richard, MD. *Cosmic Consciousness*, Penguin Books New York, 1901.

K. Sohail

Dreamers

He was born in a city
    where dreamers were
        either hanged or crucified
           and years later
               their statues were erected
                  in the four corners of the city
He used to wonder
    if dreamers knew
        they would be hanged or crucified
        why did they share
           their dreams with others?
Whenever he asked this question
    he was always told
        in this city
           not only is dreaming a sin
               asking questions is prohibited too
When he studied
    the lives of those dreamers
        he found out
           some were poets, others philosophers
           some were scientists, others saints.

From Islam to Secular Humanism

He never met any of them
>   for they had all been turned into
>   statues.

As he grew older
>   he wished he could dream, too.
>   First he felt scared
>   but then
>   the desire became so strong
>   that he waited day and night
>   to have a dream.

Finally one night
>   his wish came true!
>   He dreamt that
>   he was a fish
>   swimming in his mother's womb.
>   He had water all around him;
>   gradually
>   that body of water
>   kept on expanding and growing,
>   turned into an ocean.
>   His mother
>   became Mother Earth
>   and one fish
>   multiplied into hundreds and
>   thousands of fish.

Those fish
>   lived and swam happily in the ocean
>   but then
>   they saw some islands

K. Sohail

                and dreamt of
                    walking on those islands—
                        at that time
                            the vastness of the ocean felt smaller
Finally some fish
    jumped out of the water,
        became turtles
        and wandered around the islands.
Gradually those turtles
    turned into dozens of kinds of animals,
        those islands
            turned into jungles.
                The animals lived happily in those
                    jungles
                        until
                            they saw trees and mountains
                                and dreamt of flying
                                    so that they could sit on
                                        tree branches and mountain tops.
They started to jump,
    their legs became wings, and
        they turned into birds
        and flew everywhere.
Some birds
    dreamt of
        embracing the sun, moon and the stars
        so they flew higher and higher
            turned into clouds
                and wandered around in the skies.

From Islam to Secular Humanism

Finally those clouds
    started missing their Mother Earth
        felt lonely
           and cried,
              their tears turned into raindrops.
When those clouds
    touched mountain tops
        they became snow
           and cold winds transformed them
              into snowmen.
They started living on mountains
    like men and women
        had children and families.
           When they saw their children
              shivering in the cold
                  their hearts melted.
                    They descended to the valleys
                        as rivers
                            where they divided into tribes—
                        each tribe like each river
                            had a name and an identity.
But those names and identities
    made their lives miserable.
        Words
            created ethnic, linguistic, and religious
                differences
                so in spite of being children of the same father
                    they became enemies
                        and fought wars for centuries.

K. Sohail

But then
>   in every nation and tribe
>   some people were born
>   who were dreamers
>   some were poets, others philosophers
>   some were scientists, others saints.
>   They told their people
>   "Our stories have
>   similar beginnings
>   and similar endings.
We started our journey
>   in the ocean
>   and if we keep on flowing
>   in our ethnic, linguistic and
>   religious rivers
>   we will all meet
>   in the ocean of humanity.
>   As we evolve
>   we will transform into Gods.
>   Let's dream together
>   as Gods are the only beings
>   that can dream."
But those people
>   did not like what they heard
>   so they
>   either hanged the dreamers, or crucified them,
>   their poets and philosophers, scientists
>   and saints
>   whose statues now stand

From Islam to Secular Humanism

in the four corners of the city.
When the river
　joined the ocean
　　he saw the same hundreds and thousands of fish
　　he had seen before
　　　that ocean
　　　　gradually shrank,
　　　　　fish disappeared,
　　　　　　and he became a small fish again.
　　　　　　　Mother Earth
　　　　　　　　turned into the womb of his mother
　　　　　　　　he felt as if
　　　　　　　　　God was soon to be born.
When he awoke
　he felt blessed
　　he had had his dream!
　　　But he also knew
　　　　if he shared that dream
　　　　　what his fate would be.

K. *Sohail*

Plato is dear to me, but dearer still is truth.
                                    ~ Aristotle